LITERARY
LANDSCAPES

LITERARY LANDSCAPES

Photographed by

Michael J Stead

Lennard Publishing
1989

DEDICATION

*For Colenso Stead, my grandfather, who died long before I embarked on my photographic
career, but who will always be my greatest inspiration and example as to how I should
conduct my professional and personal life – with integrity, honesty, and passion.*

*And also for Eric Kitching, my long time film processor, who sadly died during the
production of this book. He was a good friend, and I shall greatly miss our marathon
discussions, his advice and his ideas.*

Lennard Publishing
a division of Lennard Books Ltd,
Musterlin House, Jordan Hill Road, Oxford OX2 8DP

British Library Cataloguing in Publication Data
Stead, Michael J.
Literary Landscapes.
1. English literature, Special subjects, Places – Anthologies
I. Title
820.8'032
ISBN 1 85291 065 8

First published 1989 © Michael J. Stead 1989

Designed by Cooper-Wilson
Typeset by Jigsaw Graphics
Printed and bound in Scotland
by The Eagle Press plc, Glasgow

CONTENTS

INTRODUCTION

The first seeds of *Literary Landscapes* were sown during a particularly frustrating week in the late summer of 1985. I was staying with John Hillaby at his isolated cottage high on the North Yorkshire Moors. The purpose of the expedition was to obtain suitable photographs for the cover of his book, *Hillaby's Yorkshire*. Sadly, the work of landscape photographers is often hampered by weather that adheres to the rules of Murphy's Law: we invariably get sunshine when what we want is fog, rain, or storm-clouds, and vice versa. The week in question proved to be no exception.

There was nothing to do but sit it out, and spend hours fruitlessly scanning the skies for a patch of blue. During this time, we spent many hours discussing all manner of subjects. I use the word 'discuss' loosely – it was John who would talk, relating stories from his vast wealth of knowledge. I would sit and listen in awe. One story in particular, about the time he spent at Gavin Maxwell's whaling station off Skye, intrigued me, for it located the real setting of the legendary Camusfeàrna in *Ring of Bright Water*. As it was an area I knew quite well, I was able to visualise the backdrop against which his enthralling tale of otters was played. A story I had read and loved suddenly became much more vivid and enjoyable.

I whiled away the hours thinking of other novels set in British landscapes, and how I might weave them together with photographs. Then, as happens, the idea was filed away and not developed.

My interest in it was re-awakened towards the end of my work on *Wogan's Ireland*, during a visit to a writer friend of mine. In conversation, I happened to make an innocuous remark about the inability of many people to accept photography as an art form. This had long been a bone of contention with me, more so since the advent of the newer, electronic, all-doing cameras had strengthened some beliefs that it took no particular talent to produce a photograph. My friend, in mischievous mood, taunted me by playing devil's advocate. After all, the ability to point a box, press a button, and merely record what was already in front of you took no artistic ability. Now a writer – that was different, he said. He only had words to create an atmospheric painting so vivid and real that it would induce a three-dimensional picture in the reader's mind. I know that these statements provoked a light-hearted argument which, though I can't remember whether I won or lost, was serious enough to set me researching a possible theme which would allow literature and photography to join successfully in an appreciation of the British landscape.

My first step was to find novels and poems which described some part of the landscape, and for this I was indebted to the compilers of *The Oxford Literary Guide to the British Isles*. This told me which novels used places as a backdrop, where the author had found his inspiration – invariably a place he had either visited or lived in – whether the place had been given a fictional name, or no name at all. I then had to find suitable passages, a task which I thought would be relatively easy when I embarked upon it. In reality, it meant reading some 150 novels and 200 poems, which, though thoroughly enjoyable, left me mentally drained, having not read in such quantity since my schooldays. Many of the obscure novels proved quite elusive, but thanks to the local library, almost all were eventually traced and obtained.

Then came the problems of making the final selection. I knew that, whichever I chose, there would be inevitable criticism, particularly since I would be making decisions without regard to the authors' fame. I had no intention of my photographs being purely illustrative of the text. Indeed I knew that in some cases I would not be fortunate enough to find the place, even after numerous visits, in identical conditions to the passage (I was thinking particularly of Bram Stoker's storm); nor would I, on one piece of film, be able to capture those descriptions which were of a 360-degree panorama.

Having no pretensions to being a literary critic, I finally picked those passages which, upon reading, produced – either from a fragment or from the whole – a strong emotional response and conjured up a vivid image in my mind. The further suggestion, by Adrian Stephenson at Lennard Publishing, that I write a text explaining why each passage was chosen, and how I progressed during the photographic production, was perhaps the most daunting prospect of all. I persevered, however, and the results are there for the reader to judge.

For the technically inclined, the majority of the work was produced on a 6x6 medium format camera of quite early vintage. The old mechanical Bronica S2a is far more reliable than electronic versions, in the conditions I often encounter. I have tried the company's newer models, but was less enthralled by the importer's attitude when, after two weeks, the camera refused to function. Though this is my main camera, I do use a 35mm Minolta as back-up, usually with a wide angle attached, which was used for the remaining work. As I do not, and have never used filters to create scenes artificially, the only other gadget in my camera case is patience, used in searching for the perspective of greatest impact, then waiting for Mother Nature to out-gun the filter freaks. It's probably the best accessory a landscape photographer can carry.

NORTH YORKSHIRE MOORS

The farm house lay in the shelter of a very slight green hollow, scarcely scooped out of the pasture field by which it was surrounded: the short crisp turf came creeping up the very door and windows, without any attempt at a yard or garden. . . .

High above the level of the sea towered the purple crags, whose summits were crowned with green sward that stole down the sides of the scaur a little way in grassy veins. Here and there a brook forced from the heights down to the sea, making its channel into a valley more or less broad in long process of time. And in the moorland hollows, as in these valleys, trees and underwood grew and flourished; so that, while on the bare swells of the high land you shivered at the waste desolation of the scenery, when you dropped into these 'wooded' bottoms you were charmed with the nestling shelter which they gave. But above and around these rare and fertile vales there were moors for many a mile, here and there bleak enough, with the red freestone cropping out above the scanty herbage; then, perhaps, there was a brown tract of peat and bog, uncertain footing for the pedestrian who tried to make a short cut to his destination; then on the higher sandy soil there was the purple ling, or commonest species of heather growing in wild luxuriance. . . .

I spent many days travelling around my native part of the world looking for an
illustration to fit the inspiration I drew from this passage. Towards the end I became quite
desperate, scouring mile after mile of moorland. Several friends thought I had
taken up rare bird watching, as I muttered incessantly about the 'elusive wooded bottom'.
One thought that I was succumbing to the temptation of strange perversions,
which he believed to be the result of photographing young ladies in various states of
undress. Trying to remember when I had last taken that step to corruption,
I opened a very cobwebbed trapdoor in my store of locations, which eventually led me to
the ideal place. The problem was that I knew the area a little too well, and in
my quest for originality had overlooked the obvious.

ROBIN HOOD'S BAY
North Yorkshire

From there one had a bird's eye view of the village itself. It lay compact in a ravine, whose north-east side was the protecting sea-cliff, and its cottages were so closely packed together the tiled roofs were almost continuous, making a great block of red against the blue of the sea: a red slightly veiled by the pearly haze of smoke.

Seawards of the wall the half bared backs of the twin reefs or 'scaurs' which form the comparative sheltered lagoon known as the landing, were becoming vaguely discernible. It seemed that the sound of the surf was steadily growing stronger. It travelled with a peculiar clarity on the windless air, as sound travels in an empty church, and above its deep monotonous thunder there rose at intervals a harsher, more sinister note, as though the moving sea was growing tight and thick, and the sharp rocks were splitting it like canvas.

We walked up the slipway into the dock, where Bramblewick's only two streets, Bridge Street and Chapel Street, converge in a comparatively open space; where the cobles are hauled up in very wild weather, and the lifeboat house has a convenient site.

Of all the villages perched on the North Yorkshire coast, there is an endearing quality peculiar to Robin Hood's Bay. Its individual charm has always been a magnet to artists working in every medium. In the heady flower-power days of the late Sixties it had a hippy community. Now it has its own range of creative individuals producing ornamental crafts, from carving in jet to putting ships in bottles.
It has always had that air of a close community which must derive from its days as a thriving fishing port. The novel very successfully transfers this essence to its pages, and much of its action centres around the slipway and the 'scaurs'. The actual illustration I desired meant walking outwards in the direction of the sea.
However, I wanted to balance these two essential ingredients, so that neither of them became too prominent at the other's expense. It took a great deal of pacing backwards and forwards until I felt I had the correct balance, which, as it turned out, only included a small part of the beginnings of the reef.

WHITBY HARBOUR
North Yorkshire

Then without warning the tempest broke. With a rapidity which, at the time, seemed incredible, and even afterwards is impossible to realise, the whole aspect of nature at once became convulsed. The waves rose in growing fury, each overtopping its fellow, till in a very few minutes the lately glassy sea was like a roaring and devouring monster. White crested waves beat madly on the level sands and rushed up the shelving cliffs: others broke over the piers and with their spume swept the lanthorns of the light-houses which rise from the end of either pier of Whitby harbour. The wind roared like thunder, and blew with such force that it was with difficulty that even strong men kept their feet, or clung with grim clasp to the iron stanchions. It was found necessary to clear the entire piers from the mass of onlookers, or else the fatalities of the night would have increased manifold. To add to the difficulties and dangers of the time, masses of sea fog came drifting inland – white, wet clouds, which swept by in ghostly fashion, so dank and damp and cold that it needed but little effort of imagination to think that the spirits of those lost at sea were touching their living brethren with the clammy hands of death, and many a one shuddered as the wreaths of sea mist swept by.

*Stoker presents us with the nightmarish image of nature at its most demonic,
disturbing the souls of the dead with its turbulence. The mighty storm is a portent of the
unleashing of a greater evil – the Prince of Darkness. I knew I wouldn't
be able to illustrate this literally – I certainly hoped I wouldn't. I did want at least to be
present during a storm, since our north-eastern coast is often ravaged by wind
and sea. Instead, it turned out to be one of the mildest winters we have ever experienced.
I needed a screaming sea: it hardly raised a whimper, except for once, when
I was four hundred miles away in Cornwall. So you must imagine a threatening sky
overhead, waves crashing over the piers, spray and rain beating against the
iron supports, and there floundering between them a vessel, deserted save for the headless
body lashed tightly to the wheel, swaying in the wind. . . .*

GORDALE SCAR
North Yorkshire

On the cliff above hung a few goats: one of them danced and scratched an ear with its hind foot in a place where I would not have stood stockstill 'for all beneath the moon' and as I advanced the crags seemed to close in, but I discovered a narrow entrance turning to the left between them. I followed my guide a few paces, and lo, the hills opened again into no large space, and then all farther away is barred by a stream, that at a height of about fifty feet gushes from a hole in the rock, and spreading in large sheets over its black front dashes from steep to steep, and then rattles away in a torrent down the valley . . . it is to the right, under which you stand to see the fall, that forms the principal horror of the place . . . one black solid mass . . . overshadows half the area below with its dreadful canopy . . . the drops which perpetually distil its brow, fell on my head . . . there are loose stones which hang in air, and threaten visibly . . . I stayed there (not without shuddering) a full quarter of an hour, and thought my trouble richly paid, for the impression will last for life.

There is something very provocative and frightening about this place. I already knew it quite well from previous expeditions, and understood perfectly how the writer must have felt. Apart from pot-holing, it is the only time I have become mildly claustrophobic. The knowledge that this was once a cavern, the roof of which had fallen in, added to my fears. It is a stunning indication of the capabilities of rock formation. There is a threatening prehistoric atmosphere here which incites excitement, and a belief that if sabre-toothed tigers or hairy mammoths still ruled the earth, they would choose this place for their confrontations. It is also one of those well-photographed places, and the originality of an aerial panorama, taken from a position suspended only by ropes, did not appeal to me! However, the rock formations, to me weird and eerie, reflect the ambience of the scar.

MALHAM COVE
North Yorkshire

Then he went down three hundred feet of limestone terraces, one below the other, as straight as if a carpenter had ruled them with his ruler and cut them out with his chisel. There was no heath there, but – first, a little slope, covered with the prettiest flowers, rockrose and saxifrage, and thyme and basil, and all sorts of sweet herbs.

Then bump down a two-foot step of limestone.

Then another bit of grass and flowers.

Then bump down a one foot step.

Then another bit of grass and flowers for fifty yards, as steep as the house roof, where he had to slide down on his dear little tail.

Then another step of stone, ten feet high; and there he had to stop himself, and crawl along the edge to find a crack; for if he had rolled over, he would have rolled right into the old woman's garden, and frightened her out of her wits.

You would have been giddy, perhaps, at looking down; but Tom was not. He was a brave little chimney sweep; and when he found himself on the top of a high cliff, instead of sitting down and crying for his baba (though he never had any baba to cry for) he said, 'Ah, this will just suit me' though he was very tired; and down he went, by stock and stone, sedge and ledge, bush and rush, as if he had been born a jolly little black ape, with four hands instead of two.

And all the while he never saw the Irishwoman coming behind him. But he was getting terribly tired now. The burning sun on the fells had sucked him up; but the damp heat of the woody crag sucked him up still more: and the perspiration ran out of the ends of his fingers and toes, and washed him cleaner than he had been for a whole year. But, of course, he dirtied everything terribly as he went. There has been a great black smudge all down the crag ever since.

Bump, slide, bump, may well have been the way Tom descended, but from where I stood for this illustration it would have been drop, scream, splat. I say stood, when I should have said lay: out from the rock face along a horizontally growing tree, which thankfully had not been weakened by the onslaught of time and the elements. I often have to take calculated risks to achieve a slightly different or exciting viewpoint, but this time it was a case of necessity. The day conditions seemed perfect for photography – they were also perfect for walking, picnicking, rock climbing and abseiling. . . . The cove didn't look quite right with lots of Toms and Tomesses hanging from ropes in brightly coloured attire. You can't ask someone dangling 100 feet from a ledge if they can move for 1/125th of a second or so, which meant that I had to find a place which provided natural masking of these bodies.

HAWORTH MOOR
Yorkshire

'Wuthering' being a significant provincial adjective, descriptive of the atmospheric tumult to which its station is exposed in stormy weather. Pure bracing ventilation they must have up there at all times, indeed. One may guess the power of the north wind blowing over the edge by the excessive slant of a few stunted firs at the end of the house, and by a gaunt range of ferns all stretching their limbs one way, as if craving alms of the sun. . . .

On that bleak hill top the earth was hard with a black frost and the air made me shiver through every limb. . . .

On an afternoon in October or the beginning of November – a fresh watery afternoon, when the turf and paths were rustling with moist, withered leaves, and the cold blue sky was half hidden by clouds – dark grey streamers, rapidly mounting from the west and boding abundant rain. . . .

*I was faced with two immediate problems with this passage. The first was that
Emily Brontë rarely described the landscape, preferring to portray its attributes through
her characters. Hence the rugged, mean and moody Heathcliff came to
symbolise the moorland. The second problem was the thriving commercial success of the
Brontë industry – the whole area has been saturated, photographically, from
every conceivable angle. Some years ago, my tutors told me that although photography
was only a hundred years old, it had already reached the point where the only
breakthroughs left were in technology rather than technique. Today it is a process of
adapting what has gone before to your own style. The wide angle and low
viewpoint of this shot were adopted to create drama, and it needed a long cold wait before
the clouds assembled to form an atmosphere of bleak isolation – the same
bleak isolation that Emily Brontë portrays in* Wuthering Heights.

HAWORTH MOOR
Yorkshire

There are great moors behind and on each hand of me: there are waves of mountains far beyond that deep valley at my feet. The population here must be thin. . . .

It was a very grey day: a most opaque sky, 'onding on snaw', canopied all: then flakes fell at intervals, which settled on the hard path and on the hoary lea without melting.

How different had this scene looked when I viewed it laid out beneath the iron sky of winter, stiffened in frost, shrouded with snow – when mists as chill as death wandered to the impulse of east winds along those purple peaks, and rolled down 'ing' and holm till they blended with the frozen fog of the beck.

There are inevitable similarities in all the landscapes of the Brontë sisters'
novels, so I wanted to show a different aspect of the moorland, while still depicting the
hostility which underlies their literary portraits. As I had already created the
mood with darkening skies in the illustration for Wuthering Heights, *I felt that a bright*
photograph was in order. Sunshine rarely brings out threatening qualities in a
subject, however, so the only way to retain this feeling of barrenness in such conditions
was to wait for the snow, particularly a light fall, as a landscape with its features
just breaking through is usually more interesting than a 'whiteout'. Also, at these times,
there tend to be very exciting cloud formations.

DOVEDALE
Derbyshire

That rich, undulating district of Loamshire to which Hayslope belonged lies close to a grim outskirt of Stonyshire, overlooked by its barren hills as a pretty blooming sister may sometimes be seen linked in the arm of a rugged, tall, swarthy brother; and in two or three hours' ride the traveller might exchange a bleak treeless region, intersected by lines of cold grey stone, for one where his road wound under the shelter of woods, or up swelling hills, muffled with hedgerows and long meadow-grass and thick corn; . . .

High up against the horizon were the huge conical masses of hill, like giant mounds intended to fortify this region of corn and grass against the keen and hungry winds of the north; not distant enough to be clothed in purple mystery, but with sombre greenish sides visibly specked with sheep, whose motion was only revealed by memory, not detected by sight; wooed from day to day by the changing hours, but responding with no change in themselves – left for ever grim and sullen after the flush of morning, the winged gleams of the April noonday, the parting crimson glory of the summer sun.

This passage intrigued and attracted me by its comparison between two very distinct and different landscapes, and how they enhanced each other. It also symbolises one of the great virtues of these islands where we have such rich variety, topographically, within a relatively small expanse. My research led me to the well-known Dovedale which is, in fact, a gorge. In the circumstances, it proved impossible to put both the undulating rich pasture and the grim barrenness onto one piece of emulsion. The fame with which that one part of the dale is now bestowed often belies the fact that it is really quite extensive, and the rest is as beautiful, though perhaps not immediately as awe-inspiring. I wandered far, heading towards the source of the River Dove where the contrast portrayed in the text becomes more pronounced and obvious.

CROMFORD
Derbyshire

The curving, sweeping hillsides dropped down into the narrow little valley where the noisy river, the rapid brown brook, and the white turnpike, with its jingling carts and dusty trudging wayfarers made a pretence of bustle and talk. Then up they climbed, through quiet hollows and dimpled coombs, past little woods and ridged plough-land and soft singing streams, to the heights where the great rocks lay bare and the wind lashed the torn beeches and ragged thorns. Little flowery fields of every shape and size, square fields, triangles, fish-shaped fields with odd corners, rhomboids, bounded by green hedgerows and black walls, linked arms and ran up hill and down dale, round the folded hills out of sight into countless valleys beyond where the sun set. Woods sprang up everywhere, little fairy woods of silver birches in the dells, bouquets of beech trees, neat and compact on the small rounded hills, witch woods with streaming hair on the hill-tops, and hundreds of acres of great oak and beech which followed the curves of the land and spread up to the sky. Everywhere green ribbons of lanes and paths, threaded the fields and woods, joining valley to valley, tying farm to farm, creeping over the high hills and loitering by the river. Many of these lanes that ran along the crests of the land were the old pack roads; some of them had been traversed by the Romans when they worked the mines which honeycombed the more distant hills, and some were older still, as the savage monoliths and green tumuli in the upland fields attested. As one looked across the valley, the far villages, hidden among trees in the hollows, could only be distinguished by the faint blue smoke which hung above them, a soft mist against the rolling green.

I felt that a too-clever composition or use of the weather would not be suitable in this instance, as a straightforward panoramic view would be ideal to illustrate this superbly detailed description of the countryside. However, I did not want it to be that simple, so I seized upon 'the heights where the great rocks lay bare' as my standpoint, the climb at least involving some labour. Eventually, this illustration caused me to put more thought into the composition than I originally anticipated, as an idyllic landscape would not be so idyllic with modern stone quarries scarring the hillsides.

MOORGREEN RESERVOIR
Eastwood, Nottinghamshire

When the sisters came to Willey Water, the lake lay all grey and visionary, stretching into the moist, translucent vista of trees and meadow. Fine electric activity in sound came from the dumbles below the road, the birds piping one against the other, and water mysteriously plashing, issuing from the lake. . . .

One morning the sisters were sketching by the side of Willey Water, at the remote end of the lake. Gudrun had waded out to a gravelly shoal, and was seated like a Buddhist, staring fixedly at the water – plants that rose succulent from the mud of the low shores. What she could see was mud, soft, oozy, watery mud, and from its festering chill, water plants rose up, thick and cool and fleshy, very straight and turgid, thrusting out their leaves at right angles, and having dark lurid colours, dark green and blotches of black – purple and bronze. . . .

The lake was blue and fair, the meadows sloped down in sunshine on one side, the thick dark woods dropped steeply on the other. The little pleasure launch was fussing out from the shore, twanging its music, crowded with people, flapping its paddles. . . . And on the high road, some of the common people were standing along the hedge, looking at the festivity beyond, enviously, like souls not admitted to paradise.

Lawrence uses this location in various guises throughout his novels. In Women In Love, it is bright and merry at one moment, dark and sombre the next. On my arrival at the lake, I embarked upon a very enjoyable walk. It would have been easy to depict the bright face of the lake, as such scenes presented themselves at regular intervals along the shore, but I was more interested in the oozy, dark, lurid passage of water.
I was rewarded by this illustration of what probably inspired the author to write the middle excerpt. The murky features of the lake must have contributed to the real-life tragedy upon which the drowning sequence in the novel is based.

GAINSBOROUGH
River Trent, Lincolnshire

A wide plain, where the broadening Floss hurries on between its green banks to the sea, and the loving tide, rushing to meet it, checks its passage with an impetuous embrace. On this mighty tide the black ships – laden with the fresh-scented fir planks, with rounded sacks of oil-bearing seed, or with the dark glitter of coal – are borne along to the town of St Ogg's, which shows its aged, fluted red roofs and the broad gables of its wharves between the low wooded hill and the river brink, tinging the water with soft purple hue under the transient glance of this February sun. Far away on each hand stretch the rich pastures and the patches of dark earth, made ready for the seed of broad-leaved green crops, or touched already with the tint of the tender-bladed autumn-sown corn. There is a remnant still of the last year's golden clusters of beehive ricks rising at intervals beyond the hedgerows; and everywhere the hedgerows are studded with trees: the distant ships seem to be lifting their masts and stretching their red-brown sails close among the branches of the spreading ash.

This novel has a distinctive split personality. The mill itself is probably based on one in Warwickshire, whereas St Ogg's on the Floss is Gainsborough on the Trent. The river is predominantly man-made, and its banks therefore resemble a canal. This in itself is not very photogenic, in addition to which the river no longer seems to carry the amount of traffic that passed along it in Eliot's era. Fortunately the section which particularly interested me, the red building wharves, are still intact in places. I had decided to give this illustration impact through the contrast of colour rather than through detail. Consequently, an evening sun was used to accentuate the redness against a blue sky.

MABLETHORPE SANDS
Lincolnshire

Here often, when a child, I lay reclined,
I took delight in this locality.
Here stood the infant Ilion of the mind,
And here the Grecian ships did seem to be.
And here again I come, and only find
The drain-cut levels of the marshy lea, –
Grey sandbanks, and pale sunsets, – dreary wind,
Dim shores, dense rains, and heavy clouded sea!

A still salt pool, locked in with bars of sand,
Left on the shore; that hears all night
The plunging sea draw backward from the land
Their moon-led waters white.

As the crest of some slow-arching wave,
Heard in dead of night along the table shore,
Drops flat, and after the great waters break
Whitening for half a league, and thin themselves,
Far over sands marbled with moon and sand,
From less and less to nothing.

*Anyone with a sense of belonging who comes from a seaside resort, myself included,
tends to hold their hometown in higher esteem than others of that ilk. Mablethorpe was
one of those jokes that we in Scarborough laughed at – 'I went for a day, but
it was closed', or 'The sea doesn't come in at Mablethorpe, it comes down.' I wondered
what could have possibly inspired Tennyson to write this poem. When I
arrived, the town did seem closed; paint was peeling off the deserted beach huts, and many
of the seafront arcades were boarded up – though, I have to admit, it was
January. But the beach was one of the most beautiful I have ever seen: clean, very yellow,
and rippled, and there were indeed 'salt pools locked in bars of sand'. I was
spoilt for choice – it was so easy to sense the Grecian ships of a child's mind, across the
wide expanse.*

THEDDLETHORPE
Lincolnshire

They grew warm, and walked hand in hand.

A flush came into the sky, the wan moon, half-way down the west, sank into insignificance. On the shadowy land things began to take life, plants with great leaves became distinct. They came through a pass in the big, cold sandhills on to the beach. The long waste of foreshore lay moaning under the dawn and the sea: the ocean was a flat dark strip with a white edge. Over the gloomy sea the sky was red. Quickly the fire spread among the clouds and scattered them. Crimson burned to orange, orange to dull gold, and in a golden glitter the sun came up, dribbling fierily over the waves in little splashes, as if someone had gone along and the light had spilled from her pail as she walked.

The breakers ran down the shore in long, hoarse strokes. Tiny seagulls, like specks of spray, wheeled above the line of surf. Their crying seemed larger than they. Far away the coast reached out, and melted into the morning, the tussocky sandhills seeming to sink to a level with the beach. Mablethorpe was tiny on their right. They had alone the space of all this level shore, the sea, and the upcoming sun, the faint noise of the waters, the sharp cry of the gulls.

They had a warm hollow in the sandhills where the wind did not come. He stood looking out to sea.

Of all the novels and poems I read, this was one of the most pleasant surprises. Though simple, this passage reflected the many-coloured facets of a day's awakening. The surprise was that it came from an author who is remembered for his intimate descriptions of human relationships, rather than for the background against which they were played. From bitter experience, I prepared myself for endless early mornings waiting for Mother Nature to provide a suitable rising. A veteran of sunrises like myself is still not able to anticipate their progress, which is often illogical, and knowing I could not convey its many features in one frame, the sensible approach would have been to record continuously, and choose the best in the warmth of home. I ignored this approach, only aiming to illustrate the splashes of gold spilling from the pail – my initial inspiration – at the risk of a wasted dawn.

ALDEBURGH
Suffolk

Thus by himself compell'd to live each day,
To wait for certain hours the tide's delay;
At the same times the same dull views to see,
The bounding marsh-bank and the blighted tree;
The water only, when the tides were high,
When low, the mud half-cover'd and half-dry;
The sun-burnt tar that blisters on the planks,
And bank-side stakes in their uneven ranks;
Heaps of entangled weeds that slowly float,
As the tide rolls by the impeded boat.
When tides were neap, and, in the sultry day,
Through the tall bounding mud-banks made their way,
Which on each side rose swelling, and below
The dark warm flood ran silently and slow;
There anchoring, Peter chose from man to hide,
There hang his head, and view the lazy tide
In its hot slimy channel slowly glide. . . .

*There were several choices of illustration for this passage, all of which equally
excited me, but the one I had hoped would come to fruition is reproduced here. I wandered
about the area, taking in several possibilities, all the while looking for a solitary
tree growing on the edge of the bank. Upon finding the tree, I chose a wide-angle lens,
then moved back along the bank, until a complete reflection was present in
the channel. Unbelievable as it may seem, there was even the rotting hulk of a rowing
boat tied to the tree, though the angle required for the reflection has almost
obscured it. My return journey was embarked upon with an ecstatic gait, until I tripped
over a half-buried notice board. I was intrigued, though, on looking back, I wish
I hadn't been so curious. It seems that metallic objects in the area should be avoided –
they could be unexploded bombs. I had been walking through an MOD practice range!*

RIVER DEBEN
Suffolk

No stately villas, on thy side,
May be reflected in thy tide;
No lawn-like parks, outstretching round,
The willing loiterer's footsteps bound
By woods, that cast their leafy shade,
Or deer that start across the glade;
No ruin'd abbey, grey with years,
Upon thy marge its pile uprears;
Nor crumbling castle, valours hold,
Recalls the feudal days of old.

Nor dost thou need that such should be,
To make thee, Deben, dear to me;
Thou hast thy own befitting charms
Of quiet heath and fertile farms,
With here and there a copse to fling
Its welcome shade, where wild birds sing;
Thy meads, for flocks and herds to graze;
Thy quays and docks, where seamen raise
Their anchor, and unfurl their sail
To woo and win the favouring gale.

And, above all, for me thou hast
Endearing memories of the past!
Thy winding banks, with grass o'ergrown,
By me these forty years well known,
Where, eve or morn, 'tis sweet to rove,
Have oft been trod by those I love;
By those who, through life's by-gone hours,
Have strew'd its thorny paths with flowers,
And by thy influence made thy stream
A grateful poet's favourite theme.

Many poems, when extolling the virtues of a subject, concentrate upon its
adjacent attractions. What impressed me particularly about this piece was that the
author's love for the river was totally pure, and did not depend upon its surroundings.
In the opening verse, Barton makes the point that this river does not have the fancy
adornments on its banks which some rivers boast. It was in a swollen state when
I visited, so the waterlogged banks gave me a great deal of interesting material to work
with. The reedy clumps rearing from the blue were ideal, and the foreground
roots and wood added visual interest.

MERSEA ISLAND
Essex

Between the mouths of the Blackwater and the Colne, on the east coast of Essex, lies an extensively marshy tract veined and freckled in every part with water. It is a wide waste of debatable ground contested by sea and land, subject to incessant incursions from the former, but stubbornly maintained by the latter. At high tide the appearance is that of a vast surface of moss or Sargasso weed floating on the sea, with rents and patches of shining water traversing and dappling it in all directions. The creeks, some of considerable length and breadth, extend many miles inland, and are arteries whence branches out a fibrous tissue of smaller channels, flushed with water twice in the twenty-four hours. At noon-tides, and especially at the equinoxes, the sea asserts its royalty over this vast region, and overflows the whole, leaving standing out of the flood only the long island of Mersea, and the lesser islet, called the Ray. This latter is a hill of gravel rising from the heart of the Marshes, crowned with ancient thorntrees, and possessing, what is denied the mainland, an unfailing spring of purest water. At ebb, the Ray can only be reached from the old Roman causeway, called the Strood, over which runs the road from Colchester to Mersea Isle, connecting formerly the city of the Trinobantes with the station of the Count of Saxon shore. But even at ebb, the Ray is not approachable by land unless the sun or east wind has parched the ooze into brick; and then the way is long, tedious and tortuous, among bitter pools and over shining creeks. . . .

A more desolate region can scarce be conceived, and yet it is not without beauty.

I am often attracted to desolate waste-land, especially if it's flat, which always
presents a challenge to the photographer. It is easy to produce dull and uninteresting
photographs if the subject is bland, even under normally exciting weather conditions.
To compose a picture of a more elevated standard requires greater perception, more
thought, and perhaps most important of all, keener observation in finding a foreground
subject with which to break up the monotony. It was therefore inevitable that
Mehalah would be like a gauntlet thrown before me. A long trudge uncovered no tree,
nor a rotting boat. Then, in the distance, I spied my saviour – the remains of a
landing stage jutting into the creek.

COOLING
Thames Estuary, Kent

Ours was the marsh country, down by the river, within, as the river wound, twenty miles of the sea. My first most vivid and broad impression of the identity of things, seems to me to have been gained on a memorable raw afternoon towards evening. At such a time I found out for certain, that this bleak place overgrown with nettles was the churchyard: and that Philip Pirrip, late of this parish, and also Georgiana, wife of the above, were dead and buried: and that Alexander, Bartholomew, Abraham, Tobias, and Roger, infant children of the aforesaid were also dead and buried: and that the dark flat wilderness beyond the churchyard, intersected with dykes and mounds and gates, with scattered cattle feeding on it, was the marshes: and that the low leaded line beyond was the river: and that the distant savage lair from which the wind was rushing, was the sea: and that the small bundle of shivers growing afraid of it all and beginning to cry, was Pip.

It was a rimy morning, and very damp. I had seen the damp lying on the outside of my window, as if some goblin had been crying there all night, and using the window for a pocket handkerchief. Now I saw the damp lying on the bare hedges and spare grass, like a coarser sort of spiders' webs: hanging itself from twig to twig and blade to blade. On every rail and gate, wet lay clammy, and the marsh mist was so thick, that the wooden finger on the post directing people to our village – a direction which they never accepted, for they never came there – was invisible to me until I was quite close under it. Then as I looked up at it while it dripped, it seemed to my oppressed conscience like a phantom devoting me to the Hulks.

The mist was heavier yet when I got out on the marshes, so that instead of my running at everything, everything seemed to run at me. The gates and dykes and banks came bursting at me through the mist.

Even as a child I had never been an avid fan of Dickens. The only time I really came into contact with his work was through film and television. One of the most vivid episodes of any of his dramatised novels must be the meeting between Pip and Magwitch in the graveyard. Since my early days, it has always been a scene that makes me feel uneasy. The day I arrived, a fine drizzle evoked enough of the original atmosphere to make my perusal of the photographic possibilities proceed at a far quicker pace than usual.

DOVER BEACH
Kent

The sea is calm to-night.
   The tide is full, the moon lies fair
Upon the straits; – on the French coast the light
Gleams and is gone; the cliffs of England stand,
Glimmering and vast, out in the tranquil bay.
Come to the window, sweet is the night-air!
Only, from the long line of spray
Where the sun meets the moon-blanchd' land,
Listen! You hear the grating roar
Of pebbles which the waves draw back, and fling
At their return, up the high strand,
Begin, and cease, and then again begin,
With tremulous cadence slow, and bring
The eternal note of sadness in.

*Originally I was going to produce a literal illustration taken at the dead of
night – for some reason I changed my mind. Perhaps it was the grating of the sea against
the pebbles – in daylight unnerving, at night, unbearably eerie. Instead I risked
life and limb to include the base of the Shakespeare Cliff in the photograph.
The white chalk is very much a symbol of the freedom that we, in these islands, hold so
close to our hearts.*

WATERSHIP DOWN
Berkshire

It was the evening of the following day. The north-facing escarpment of Watership Down, in shadow since early morning, now caught the western sun for an hour before twilight. Three hundred feet the down rose vertically in a stretch of no more than six hundred – a precipitous wall, from the thin belt of trees at the foot of the ridge where the steep flattened out. The light, full and smooth, lay like a gold rind over the turf, the furze and yew bushes, the few wind-stunted thorn trees. From the ridge, the light seemed to cover all the slope below, drowsy and still. But down in the grass itself, between the bushes, in that thick forest trodden by the beetle, the spider and the hunting shrew, the moving light was like a wind that danced among them to set them scurrying and weaving.

From the summit, the apparent immobility of the vast, blue distance was broken, here and there, by wisps of smoke and tiny, momentary flashes of glass. Far below lay the fields green with wheat, the flat pastures grazed by horses, the darker greens of the woods. They too, like the hillside jungle, were tumultuous with evening, but from the remote height turned to stillness, their fierceness tempered by the air that lay between them.

Though this story was written for the author's children, it can also be read as a modern-day fable – a moral tale of the trials and tribulations that had to be endured as part of the search for a herbiferous Nirvana. Watership Down had to be portrayed as this final idyll. What does constitute Heaven to rabbits? An allotment full of lettuces? Pure guesswork assumed a little forestation for edibles, a plateau of grass for play, and old trees to provide those essential cosy love nests.

PORTLAND
Dorset

❦

At the top they turned and stood still. To the left of them the sky was streaked like a fan with the lighthouse rays, and under their front, at periods of a quarter of a minute, there arose a deep, hollow stroke like the single beat of a drum, the intervals being filled with long-drawn rattling, as of bones between huge canine jaws. It came from the vast concave of Deadman's Bay, rising and falling against the pebble dyke.

But just within the summit of the bank, whither it had apparently been hauled to be out of the way of the waves, was one of the local boats called lerrets, bottom upwards. As soon as they saw it the pair ran up the pebbly slope towards it by a simultaneous impulse. They then perceived that it had lain there a long time, and were comforted to find it capable of affording more protection than anyone would have expected from a distant view.

Nothing but the frail bank of pebbles divided them from the raging gulf without, and at every bang of the tide against it the ground shook, the shingle clashed, the spray rose vertically, and was blown over their heads. Quantities of sea-water trickled through the pebble wall, and ran in rivulets across their path to join the sea within. The 'Island' was an island still.

I have seen many interpretations of Chesil Bank, most of which show the great curve being beaten by waves and spray. My thoughts wandered to the romantic notion of two people in love, sheltering safe against the elements. The storm was undoubtedly included to enhance this. Though I wanted to make the boat the focal point of my illustration, I had to try to retain that emotional feel – I decided that a sunset was likely to involve less waiting than a storm. Trying to turn the boat the right way up proved more difficult than I imagined, so I could not be completely loyal to the description. My efforts were subsequently rewarded with two days of painful walking!

LYME COBB
Dorset

∞

...but finally because it is a superb fragment of folk-art. Primitive yet complex, elephantine yet delicate; as full of subtle curves and volumes as a Henry Moore or a Michelangelo; and pure, clean, salt, a paragon of mass. I exaggerate? Perhaps, but I can be put to the test, for the Cobb has changed very little since the year of which I write; though the town of Lyme has, and the test is not fair if you look back towards land. However, if you had turned northward and landward in 1867, as the man that day did, your prospect would have been harmonious. A picturesque congeries of some dozen or so houses and a small boat-yard – in which, arklike on its stocks, sat the thorax of a lugger – huddled at where the Cobb runs back to land. Half a mile to the east lay, across sloping meadows, the thatched and slated roofs of Lyme itself; a town that had its heyday in the Middle Ages and has been declining ever since. To the west sombre grey cliffs, known locally as Ware Cleeves, rose steeply from the shingled beach where Monmouth entered upon his idiocy. Above them and beyond, stepped massively inland, climbed further cliffs masked by dense woods. It is in this aspect that the Cobb seems most a last bulwark against all that wild eroding coast to the west.

Before reading this book, or Pride and Prejudice *in which the Cobb and Lyme*
are also described, I already had a preconceived image of the kind of illustration
I envisaged. It was probably similar to most people's image, and owing entirely to the
success of the film. Anyone who has seen it can never forget the powerful and emotional
vision of Meryl Streep, the black-garbed figure at the end of the Cobb, braving the raging
sea. But I wanted the author's words to instill the ideas into my mind, not someone
else's interpretation of them. However, upon reading the novel, the
problem didn't materialise – the first four lines of this passage
gave me a concrete interpretation.

TEIGN VALLEY
Chagford, Devon

The wooded valley lay under a grey and breezy forenoon; swaying alders marked each intermittent gust with a silver ripple of upturned foliage, and still reaches of the river similarly answered the wind with hurrying flickers and furrows of dimpled light. Through its transparent flood, where the waters ran in shadow and escaped reflections, the river revealed a bed of ruddy brown and rich amber. This harmonious colouring proceeded from the pebbly bottom, where a medley of warm agate tones spread and shimmered, like some far reaching mosaic beneath the crystal. Above Teign's shrunken current extended oak and ash, while her banks bore splendid recourse of the wild water-loving dwellers in that happy valley. Meadowsweet nodded creamy crests: hemlock and fool's parsley and seeding willow-herb crowded together beneath far scattered filigree of honey suckles and brambles with berries, some ripe, some red; while the scarlet corals of briar and white briony gemmed every riotous trailing thicket, dene and dingle along the rivers brink: and in the grassy spaces between, rose little chrysoprase steeples of wood sage all set in shining fern.

The attraction of this passage was that it portrays a typical English river scene,
loved by so many of us, where families picnic on hot sunny days, where children can
safely paddle about on the colourful river bed. Teign Valley itself is very beautiful and is
a perfect example of what can be achieved without excessive commercial enterprise. Well
laid-out paths meander in both directions along the river, and after
such energetic exercise, you can unwind in a cafe or pub.

DARTMOOR
Devon

Presently he stood on the side of lofty Steeperton and surveyed the vast valley known as Taw Marsh, which lies between the western foothills of Cosden Beacon and the Belstone Tors to the north. The ragged manes of the latter hills wind through the valley in one lengthy ridge, and extend to a tremendous castellated mass of stone, by name Oke Tor. This erection, with its battlements and embrasures, outlying scarps and counterscarps, remarkably suggests the deliberate and calculated creation of man. It stands upon a little solitary hill at the head of Taw Marsh, and wins its name from the East Okement river which runs through the valley on its western flank. Above wide fen and marsh it rises, yet seen from Steeperton's vaster altitude, Oke Tor looks no greater than some fantastic child castle built by a Brobdingnagian baby with granite bricks. Below it on this July day the waste of bogland was puckered with brown tracts of naked soil, and seamed and scarred with peat cuttings. Here and there drying turves were propped in pairs and dotted the hillsides; a single curlew, with rising and falling crescendos of sound, flew here and there under needless anxiety, and far away on White Hill and the enormous breast of Cosden, glimmered grey stone ghosts from the past – track-lines and circles and pounds – the work of those Children of the Mist who laboured here when the world was younger, whose dust now lay under the newborn light of the budding heath.

What struck me about this passage was the end of the chapter from which
it was taken. The narrator strays into a military firing range, and dire
consequences follow. Oh dear! I thought, while tracing the route on a map:
the tors mentioned were indeed adjacent to the Okement firing range, and the slightest
deviation from the path, or even a wrong turning, would put me slap-bang in the middle
of it. On making enquiries, I was assured that firing times were posted all along
the moor. This knowledge did little to abate my fears. On the day of my excursion,
I bought four newspapers, just to ensure that there had been no printing
errors, and triple-checked three different notices.

CORNISH QUARRY
Penpethy Quarries, near Delabole

It happened once, before the duller
  Loomings of life defined them,
I searched for slates of greenish colour
    A quarry where men mined them:

And saw, the while I peered around there,
    In the quarry standing
A form against the slate background there,
    Of fairness eye-commanding.

And now, though fifty years have flown me,
    With all their dreams and duties,
And strange-pipped dice my hand has thrown me,
    And dust are all her beauties.

Green slates – seen high on roofs, or lower
    In waggon, truck, or lorry –
Cry out: 'Our home was where you saw her
    Standing in the quarry!'

*I found the notion of the poem so romantic. To be reminded of love by
something as mundane and commonplace as slates. I was also intrigued by the description
of the colour of the slates – I had always thought of them as grey. Are grey
slate roofs just a trick of the light? Come to that, is flesh pink? The predominant colour
is, in fact, green. It only becomes obvious in darkness – look at the shadowed
areas of the face and hands. So it was with the slates. This greenness was apparent in
various quarries. It only took a short time to find a suitable graphic effect for
the photograph, though I did spend a little longer there than was necessary, sliding down
the slate piles.*

CORNISH CLIFFS

The sea runs back against itself
  With scarcely time for breaking wave
To cannonade a slatey shelf
And thunder under in a cave

Before the next can fully burst.
The headwind, blowing harder still,
Smooths it to what it was at first –
A slowly rolling water-hill.

Against the breeze the breakers haste,
Against the tide their ridges run
And all the sea's a dappled waste
Criss-crossing underneath the sun.

Far down the beach the ripples drag
Blown backward, rearing from the shore,
And wailing gull and shrieking shag
Alone can pierce the ocean roar.

Unheard, a mongrel hound gives tongue,
Unheard are shouts of little boys:
What chance has any inland lung
Against this multi-water noise?

Here where the cliffs alone prevail
I stand exultant, neutral, free,
And from the cushion of the gale
Behold a huge consoling sea.

Betjeman wrote a great many poems about the Port Isaac area. My original concept was to capture the atmosphere of the whole piece, but this was not to be. I tracked the coastal path in very dull weather, then made a decision to resort to my second plan – to illustrate the slate shelf cliffs as I back-tracked. I was nearing my starting point late in the afternoon, when I detected the possibility of a break in the cloud blanket. In anticipation, I selected a standpoint that gave me a sweeping view of the cliffs. Although I perched on a cliff edge, I was reasonably safe as a strong wind was blowing inland, but I'm glad I don't suffer from vertigo – from the cliff there was a 300-foot drop down to the rocks. In a scene like this, it is inevitable that film cannot cope with the extreme range of tones, so I bracketed exposures from readings taken from the highlights on the sea and the dark cliff face. From the results, I then chose the most suitable frame which gave some detail in both areas, although it is inevitable that one or the other has suffered some loss of detail.

TINTAGEL
Cornwall

The year lies fallen and faded
On cliffs by clouds invaded,
With tongues of storms upbraided,
With wrath of waves bedinned:
And inland, wild with warning,
As in deaf ears or scorning,
The clarion even and morning
Rings of the south-west wind.

The wild bents wane and wither
In blasts whose breath bows hither
Their grey-grown heads and thither,
Unblest of rain or sun:
The pale fierce heavens are crowded
With shapes like dreams beclouded,
As though the old year enshrouded
Lay, long ere life were done.

Full charged with oldworld wonders,
From dusk Tintagel thunders
A note that smites and sunders
The hard frore fields of air:
A trumpet stormier sounded
That once from lists rebounded
When strong men sense-confounded
Fell thick in tourney there.

*This is the only piece of literature I decided to use that provoked an emotion
unaccompanied by any visual image. I almost discarded it for this reason, but every time
I read the poem, it seemed to draw me with its unearthly quality. So I decided
at least to instigate a search which, since it was on the same coast as Betjeman's Cornish
cliffs, could be initiated at the same time. The weather frustrated me until late
afternoon, but as I neared the far point of my walk, above Tintagel, I noticed a rocky
bulk in the bay, and perhaps more importantly, light conditions producing
colours which I thought unnatural. I had no hesitation in scrambling down the banks for
this photograph; the effect seemed to tie in with my emotions about the poem.*

BODMIN MOOR
Cornwall

It was a silent desolate country though, vast and untouched by human hand; on the high tors the slabs of stone leant against one another in strange shapes and forms, massive sentinels who had stood there since the hands of God first fashioned them.

Some were shaped like giant furniture, with monstrous chairs and twisted tables; and sometimes the smaller crumbling stones lay on the summit of the hill like a giant himself, his huge, recumbent form darkening the heather and the coarse tufted grass. There were long stones that stood on end, balancing themselves in a queer miraculous way, as though they leant against the wind; and there were flat altar-stones whose smooth and polished surfaces stared up towards the sky, awaiting a sacrifice that never came . . . .

Strange winds blew from nowhere; they crept along the surface of the grass, and the grass shivered; they breathed upon the little pools of rain in the hollowed stones, and the pools rippled. Sometimes the wind shouted and cried, and the cries echoes in the crevices, and moaned, and was lost again. There was a silence on the tors that belonged to another age: an age that is past and vanished as though it has never been, an age when man did not exist, but pagan footsteps trod upon the hills. And there was a stillness in the air, and a stranger, older peace, that was not the peace of God.

Can you imagine a place, created by nature, where the overwhelming feeling
is the presence of the pagan? If anywhere, that place is Bodmin Moor. The description
of the massive slabs, carved by the wind and rain, acted like a magnet to my
photographic senses. High amongst the stones on Rough Tor was a strange unearthly
world, resembling every word that Daphne Du Maurier wrote. As I wandered
around these monoliths, every hair on my body stood on end. I began to think that
capturing the scene on film had in some way invoked the wrath of the gods,
for as I was packing my equipment away, a sound of rolling thunder filled the air, the
ground began to shake, and a tormented screaming built up to an almost
unbearable pitch. I fell to my knees, my eardrums near to exploding, my heart pounding,
and buried my face in the rock. As a great shadow fell across me, I looked to
the sky, only to see a military jet pass a mere fifty feet above me!

CLOVELLY
Devon

∾

There was no road in it, there was no wheeled vehicle in it, there was not a level yard in it. From the sea-breach to the cliff top two irregular rows of white houses, placed opposite to one another, and twisting here and there, and there and here, rose, like the sides of a long succession of stages of crooked ladders, and you climbed up the village, or climbed down the village by the staves between, some six feet wide or so, and made of sharp irregular stones . . . No two houses in the village were alike, in chimney, size, shape, door, window, gable, roof-tree, anything. The sides of the ladders were musical with water, running clear and bright. The staves were musical with the clattering feet of the pack-horses and pack-donkeys, and the voices of the fishermen's wives and their many children. The pier was musical with the wash of the sea, the creaking of capstans, and windlasses, and the airy fluttering of little vanes and sails. The rough, bleached sea-boulders of the shore, were brown with drying nets. The red-brown cliffs, richly wooded to their extremest verge, had their softened and beautiful forms reflected in the bluest water.

Perhaps Mr Dickens was more instrumental in first popularising Clovelly than Charles Kingsley who based his Westward Ho! *on the village, which now charges its visitors for the privilege of setting foot upon its cobbled slopes. I doubt whether the village has changed very much since this was written, except for the now-obvious signs of the tourist industry. I was anxious not to produce a picture-postcard representation. The rain, though, making the cobbles a greasy hazard, proved ideal, as it gave the stones of the village an almost ethereal quality. Even in March the streets were quite busy, causing me much frustration as I didn't wish to include a human form in the photograph. The groups were sufficiently spaced apart to keep me waiting an hour for a deserted street.*

FOREST OF DEAN
Hereford and Worcester

The quiet congregation of the trees
Awoke to a rippled whisper. The light winged breeze
Brushed leaf against leaf, softly and delicately fingering
Silken beech and ragged oak leaf: and in the cool shadow
And wavering dapple of tremulous sunlight lingering
As weary as the hot gold glow of the buttercup meadow,
And renewing his strength in the cool green and still shade
Of the forest, deeper and deeper burrowing in
By pathway and trackway the green ride and arched glade
Over hyacinth and white starred garlic and curled fern,
And dreaming in some unvisited haven to win
New life from the growing grass and rejoicing return
To sweep from hill to valley, from valley to hill.
The birds were still,
Only far off a cuckoo calling,
Drowsily and perpetually a far-off cuckoo calling.

Illustrating this passage gave me a headache, with some help from overhanging branches
– perhaps it will teach me not to become so engrossed in the search for
composition. An obvious photographic scene would be of shafts of sunlight streaming
through a glade of trees, illuminating the plant life, but at the time I visited
(through deadline necessity) the forest was in a state of undress. However, during the time
I spent teaching students of Graphics, I had become very aware of the natural
design of nature, particularly in close-up, and here was an ideal opportunity to put this
into practice. It can be very rewarding to walk with a camera, inspecting the
areas immediately above and below your path, in addition to the wider vistas.

RHONDDA VALLEY
Glamorgan

The first thing I saw was the slag heap.

Big it had grown, long, and black, without life or sign, lying along the bottom of the valley, on both sides of the river. The green grass, and the reeds and the flowers, all had gone, crushed beneath it. And every minute the burden grew, as cage after cage screeched along the cables from the pit, bumped to a stop at the tipping gear, and emptied dusty loads onto the ridged, black, dirty back.

Below us, the river ran sweet as ever, happy in the sun, but as soon as it met the darkness between the sloping walls of slag it seemed to take fright and go spiritless, smooth, black, without movement. And on the other side it came forth grey, and began to hurry again, as though anxious to get away. But its banks were stained, and the reeds and grasses that dressed it were hanging, and black, and sickly, ashamed of their dirtiness, ready to die of shame, they seemed, and of sorrow for their dear friend, the river.

This proved to be one of the more difficult illustrations. I had my image:
the pit-head rising above a village which constantly fought for space amidst the spreading
mass of underground débris, brought up from the bowels of the earth by years
of mining. I confidently carried my camera to Gilfach Goch, the scene of the novel.
Where was the pit-head? Where were the surface buildings which released
coughing, black-faced employees at the end of each shift? All I saw was a rural village,
a park and playing fields, a scenario repeated all around the valleys. It took
me a whole day to find a suitable site. The NCB should perhaps be applauded for this
reclamation and social redevelopment, but I can't help wondering if the
inhabitants would rather have the grimy stonework, the black scars, and an atmosphere
polluted with coal dust. At least these would indicate a still-thriving industry.

LAUGHARNE
Dyfed

∞

Voice of a guide book.

Less than five hundred souls inhabit the three quaint streets and the few narrow by-lanes and scattered farmsteads that constitute this small, decaying watering place which may, indeed, be called a 'backwater of life' without disrespect to its natives who possess, to this day, a salty individuality of their own. The main street, Coronation Street, consists for the most part of humble, two storied houses many of which attempt to achieve some measure of gaiety by prinking themselves out in crude colours and by the liberal use of pinkwash, though there are remaining a few eighteenth century houses of more pretension, if, on the whole in a sad state of disrepair. Though there is little to attract the hillclimber, the healthseeker, the sportsman, or the weekending motorist, the contemplative may, if sufficiently attracted to spare it some leisurely hours, find, in its several curious customs, and in the conversation of its local 'characters' some of that picturesque sense of the past so frequently lacking in towns and villages which have kept more abreast of the times.

Second Voice.

Herring gulls heckling down to the harbour where the fishermen spit and prop the morning up and eye the fishy sea smooth to the sea's end as it lulls in blue. Green and gold money, tobacco, tinned salmon, hats with feathers, pots of fish-paste, warmth for the winter to be, weave and leap in it rich and slippery in the flash and shapes of fishes through the cold sea streets. But with blue lazy eyes the fishermen gaze at the milk mild whispering water with no ruck or ripple as though it blew great guns and serpents and typhooned the town.

Many years ago, before electricity or gas came to the cobbled streets of Yorkshire, this was part of the syllabus for my English 'A'-level. Ultimately, I failed the exam, but I like to think that was more because of distractions than incapability. This author's use of language had fascinated me, and I knew before the outset that he portrayed the environment through his descriptions of people rather than places. Consequently, I decided to create a scene in which his characters could be imagined. I opted for the harbour area as the location, rather than the town, because of the speech of the second voice; and as I regarded his writing as bright, jaunty and exhilarating, I used the yellow boat to liven up the foreground.

RHAEDER DHU
The Black Falls, Gwynedd

Sometimes she descended into the bottom of the dingles, to the black rocky beds of the torrents, and dreamed away hours at the feet of the cataracts. One spot in particular, from which she had at first shrunk with terror, became by degrees her favourite haunt. A path turning and returning at acute angles, led down a steep wood-covered slope to the edge of a chasm, where a pool, or resting place of a torrent, lay far below. A cataract fell in a single sheet into the pool; the pool boiled and bubbled at the base of the fall, but through the greater part of its extent, lay calm, deep, and black, as if the cataract had plunged through it to an unimaginable depth, without disturbing its eternal repose. At the opposite extremity of the pool, the rocks almost met at their summits, the trees of the opposite banks intermingled their leaves, and another cataract plunged from the pool into a chasm, on which the sunbeams never gleamed. High above, on both sides, the steep woody slopes of the dingle soared into the sky; and from a fissure in the rock, on which the little path terminated, a single gnarled and twisted oak stretched itself over the pool, forming a fork with its boughs at a short distance from the rock. Miss Susannah often sat on the rock with her feet resting on the tree: in time, she made her seat on the tree itself, with her feet hanging over the abyss; and at length, she accustomed herself to lie along upon its trunk, with her side on the mossy bole of the fork, and an arm round one of the branches. From this position a portion of the sky and the woods was reflected in the pool, which, from its bank, was but a mass of darkness.

Finding the location that had inspired Peacock to write so picturesquely was difficult. Although it was not marked on maps, I eventually traced it through a walking guide and a helpful hiker. The road was a single track, so I pulled onto the side so as not to obstruct the highway. A sinking feeling made me aware that I might need tractor to move the car out again. The Falls were impressive, but certainly showed me the power of artistic licence at work in the passage. The black pool referred to in the text would be at one stage of the cataract higher than this – I would have needed wings to reach it!

FESTINIOG
Gwynedd

By fair Festiniog, mid the Northern Hills,
The Vales are full of beauty, and the Heights,
Thin set with mountain sheep, show statelier far
Than in the tamer South. There the stern round
Of labour rules, – a silent land, sometimes
Loud with the blast that buffets all the hills
Whereon the workers toil, in quarries hewn
Upon the terraced rocksides. Tier on tier,
Above the giddy depths, they edge and cling
Like flies to the sheer precipice as they strike
The thin cleft slate. For solace of their toil
Song comes to strengthen them, and songlike verse
In the old Cymric measures.

*As soon as I unearthed this poem, I could visualise the very scene that the
author was describing. The town was built on the slate industry, and all around and above
it tower great grey mountains of hewn slate. There are several Slate Mine
museums, but though these are excellent for education and for leisure, I found them too
contrived to use for the illustration. So I followed a path from the town into
what I assumed was still a working quarry, where the toil of man, to the great cost of the
working community, has been replaced by the work of machines. In the
stillness of evening when all work had ceased, I could almost hear the ghostly battalions
of long dead workers, their harmonious Welsh voices echoing
around the slate. The rusting carts seemed to amplify their presence, serving as a
memorial to a past way of life.*

SNOWDON
Gwynedd

There we stood on the Wyddfa, in a cold bracing atmosphere, though the day was almost stifling hot in the regions from which we had ascended. There we stood enjoying a scene inexpressibly grand, comprehending a considerable part of the mainland of Wales, the whole of Anglesey, a faint glimpse of part of Cumberland: the Irish Channel, and what might be either a misty creation or a shadowy outline of the hills of Ireland. Peaks and pinnacles and huge moels stood up here and there, about us and below us, partly in glorious light, partly in deep shade. Manifold were the objects which we saw from the brow of Snowdon, but of all the objects which we saw, those which filled us most with delight and admiration, were numerous lakes and lagoons, which, like sheets of ice or polished silver, lay reflecting the rays of the sun in the deep valleys.

Oer yw'r Eira ar Eryri, – o'ryw	Cold is the snow on Snowdon's brow
Ar awyr i rewi;	It makes the air so chill;
Oer yw'r ia ar riw 'r ri,	For cold, I trow, there is no snow
A'r Eira oer yw 'Ryri	Like that of Snowdon's hill.
O Ri y'Ryri yw'r oera, – o'r ar,	A hill most chill is Snowdon's hill
Ar oror wir arwa;	and wintry is his brow;
O'r awyr a yr Eira	From Snowdon's hill the breezes chill
O'i ryw i roi rew a'r ia	Can freeze the very snow.

*This early travel book, written before the advent of a reliable transport system,
is quite remarkable for its extensive coverage of the country. In these early days the ascent
of the mountain was a feat of endurance: today we can travel to the summit
by rail. The passage attracted me with its panoramic view, and its cold, cold snow. Out
of these two features, the elements would determine which was usable.
I ascended the Pyg track, leaving Pen y Pass in brilliant sunshine. However, upon
reaching a point known as the Zigzags, conditions changed dramatically.
Though a short steep climb would lead me to the easy ridge to the summit, a descending
party informed me that the visibility higher up was very poor. Being alone,
and not wishing this work to be published posthumously, I sat with a pork pie in one hand,
and a brandy flask in the other, and waited for the swirling mist to paint me a
picture on Snowdon's snow-capped crags.*

LLANBERIS PASS
Gwynedd

The vale contracted as they advanced, and, when they had passed the termination of the lake, their road wound along a narrow and romantic pass, through the middle of which an impetuous torrent dashed over vast fragments of stone. The pass was bordered on both sides by perpendicular rocks, broken into the wildest forms of fantastic magnificence.

'These are, indeed,' said Mr Escot, *'confracti mundi rudera'**; yet they must be feeble images of the valleys of the Andes, where the philosophic eye may contemplate, in their utmost extent, the effects of that tremendous convulsion which destroyed the perpendicularity of the poles and inundated this globe with that torrent of physical evil, from which the greater torrent of moral evil has issued, that will continue to roll on, with an expansive power and an accelerated impetus, till the whole human race shall be swept away in its vortex'. . . .

They now emerged, by a winding ascent, from the vale of Llanberis, and after some time arrived at Bedd Gelert. Proceeding through the sublimely romantic pass of Aberglaslynn . . . .

Vast rocks and precipices, intersected with little torrents, formed the barrier on the left: on the right, the triple summit of Moëlwyn reared its majestic boundary: in the depth was that sea of mountains, the wild and stormy outline of the Snowdonian chain, with the giant Wyddfa towering in the midst.

*Fragments of a demolished world

*'Confracti mundi rudera': the recitation of it conjured up grand rugged images,
and the translation merely served to add to them. I was not disappointed, for the Pass did
indeed resemble 'fragments of a demolished world', with sheer walls on one
side, and on the other, a glacier of stone frozen at some point during the destruction.
Although the vast shelf proved to be not quite as solid as it seemed from a
distance, after a precarious scramble across boulders the illustration became relatively
simple. I was even able to wave to a coachload of surprised tourists, motoring
along the valley bottom!*

BEN BULBEN
Co. Sligo

(i)

Swear by what the sages spoke
Round the Mareotic Lake
That the Witch of Atlas knew,
Spoke and set the cocks a-crow.

Swear by those horsemen, by those women
Complexion and form proved superhuman,
That pale, long-visaged company
That air in immortality
Completeness of their passions won;
Now they ride the wintry dawn
Where Ben Bulben sets the scene.

(vi)

Under bare Ben Bulben's head
In Drumcliff churchyard Yeats is laid.
An ancestor was rector there
Long years ago, a church stands near,
By the road an ancient cross.
No marble, no conventional phrase;
On limestone quarried near the spot
By his command these words are cut:

Cast a cold eye
On life, on death.
Horseman, pass by!

This poem, almost a last will and testament in which Yeats stated what was
to happen to his body after his death, was strictly adhered to. From his grave, it is quite
easy to understanding why this landscape inspired his visions. Ben Bulben's
shape, alone, is capable of evoking imaginary technicolor epics of classical scenes being
played out beneath its stoical stare. I once watched a single cloud brush the
summit and roll lazily down its slope like a great white caterpillar. Sadly, the undeveloped
film was stolen with the rest of my equipment while I was waiting for a ferry
from Dublin.

CONNEMARA LANDSCAPE

Astony stretch, grey boulders
Half-buried in furze and heather,
Purple and gold – Connemara's
Old bones dressed in colours
Out of a royal past.

Inshore the sea is marbled
And veined with foam. The Twelve Pins
Like thunderclouds hewn from rock
Or gods in a cloudy fable
Loom through an overcast.

The roofless dwellings have grown
Back to the earth they were raised from
And tune with those primordial
Outcrops of grey stone
Among the furze and the heather.

Where the man is dispossessed
Silence fills up his place
Fast as a racing tide.
Little survives of our West
But stone and the moody weather.

The last time I had been in Connemara was while producing the illustrations for Wogan's Ireland. *I have very happy memories of the entire country, but particularly of this region. It was on visits to this area that I climbed Ireland's Holy Mountain (twice, though through necessity rather than as an act of faith). It was here that I regularly got lost, since the road signs, like the inhabitants, tend to speak in the mother tongue. Here, I also had the friendliest of welcomes as I wandered through the coastal villages, or the largest peat bogs in the world. As I stalked the wild Connemara ponies (with camera only), past deserted cottages, now mere crumbling piles of stone, yet still protected by the mighty barrier of the Twelve Pins. I've a flock of fond memories, and this poem, like a shepherd, rounded them all up and brought them home. It really is impossible to do justice to the poem through one photograph, but I have tried my best.*

WIGAN
Greater Manchester

∾

A slag heap is at best a hideous thing, because it is so planless and functionless. It is something just dumped on the earth, like the emptying of a giant's dust-bin. On the outskirts of the mining towns there are frightful landscapes where your horizon is ringed completely round by jagged grey mountains, and underfoot is mud and ashes and overhead the steel cables where tubs of dirt travel slowly across miles of country. Often the slag heaps are on fire, and at night you can see the red rivulets of fire winding this way and that, and also the slow moving blue flames of sulphur, which always seem on the point of expiring and always spring out again. Even when a slag heap sinks, as it does ultimately, only an evil brown grass grows on it, and it retains its hummocky surface. One in the slums of Wigan, used as a playground, looks like a choppy sea suddenly frozen: 'the flock mattress', it is called locally. Even centuries hence when the plough drives over the places where coal was once mined, the sites of ancient slag heaps will still be distinguishable from an aeroplane.

I remember a winter afternoon in the dreadful environs of Wigan. All around was the lunar landscape of slag heaps, and to the north through the passes, as it were, between the mountains of slag, you could see the factory chimneys sending out their plumes of smoke.

I had made a decision not to include any urban or city descriptions, as the scenes they describe are likely to have been mutilated by bulldozers and replaced with monstrosities from an architect's worst nightmare since the original description was written. When I came upon this piece, written by one of my favourite authors, I began a search of Lancashire and Yorkshire, looking for the biggest, ugliest, dirtiest, most squalid blot on the landscape that I could find. This was the winner, out of a hundred possibilities! My approach towards making interesting pictures out of eyesores is to use colour variations and inherent shapes to create a graphically pleasing picture.

PENDLE HILL
Lancashire

Before setting forward, he cast a glance towards Pendle Hill, which formed the most prominent object on view on the left, and lay like a leviathan basking in the sunshine.

The vast mass rose up gradually, until at its furthest extremity it attained an altitude of more than eighteen hundred feet above the sea. At the present moment it was without a cloud, and the whole of its broad outline was distinctly visible.

'I love Pendle Hill,' cried Nicholas enthusiastically; 'and from whatever side I view it – whether from this place, where I see it from end to end, from its lowest point to its highest, from Padiham, where it frowns upon me, from Clitheroe, where it smiles, or from Downham, where it rises in full majesty before me – from all points and under all aspects, whether robed in mist or radiant in sunshine. Born beneath its giant shadow, I look upon it with filial regard. Some folks say Pendle Hill wants grandeur and sublimity, but they themselves must be wanting taste. Its broad, round, smooth mass is better than the roughest, craggiest, shaggiest, must sharply-splintered mountain of them all.' 'Every man to his taste, squire,' observed Potts, 'but to my mind, Pendle Hill has no other recommendation than its size. I think it is a great brown, ugly, lumpy mass, without beauty or form of any striking character.'

On this visit, I saw the top of Pendle Hill for the first time. I'm sure it is often bathed in glorious weather, as hundreds of walkers would no doubt testify, but until this trip I had never experienced it. Admittedly, my only visits had been on the Students' Union Hallowe'en witch-spotting excursions, when descending darkness and mist were pre-requisites for the visit. The reputed haunt of the witches is at the summit. But, witch-spotting aside, Pendle Hill certainly has a permanent air of the supernatural around its slopes, in all weathers.

SILVERDALE
Morecambe Bay, Lancashire

She crossed the field by the side of the house, ran down the steep and rocky path, and was carried by the impetus of her descent far out on the level sands – but not far enough for her intent. Without looking to the right hand or the left, where comers might have seen, she went forward to the black posts, which, rising above the heaving waters, marked where the fishermen's nets were laid. She went straight towards this place, and hardly stinted her pace even where the wet sands were glittering with the receding waves. Once there, she turned round, and in a darting glance, saw that as yet no one was near. She was perhaps half a mile or more from the grey silvery rocks, which sloped away into the brown moorland, interspersed with a field here and there of golden, waving corn. Behind were purple hills, with sharp, clear outlines, touching the sky. A little on one side from where she stood, she saw the white cottages and houses which formed the village of Abermouth, scattered up and down, and on a windy hill, about a mile inland, she saw the little grey church, where even now many were worshipping in peace.

The tide had turned; the waves were slowly receding, as if loath to lose the hold they had, so lately, and with such swift bounds, gained on the yellow sands. The eternal moan they have made since the world began filled the ear, broken only by the skirl of the grey seabirds as they alighted in groups on the edge of the waters, or as they rose up with their measured, balancing motion, and the sunlight caught their white breasts. There was no sign of human life to be seen: no boat, or distant sail, or near shrimper.

Morecambe Bay is quite familiar to me from my college days at Blackpool.
I also know the dangers of the rapid tide movements and shifting sands. The course
included completing photographic briefs simulating client demands in the
world of advertising. A friend decided that a Range Rover would look ideal on the vast,
desolate stretch of sand. He managed to borrow a vehicle, but didn't get his
shot, though he did get a large bill for a burnt-out clutch and salt-water damage.
Although my illustration of what Mrs Gaskell would have seen from the shore
was taken from a safe point, I did once have to beat a hasty retreat from the sandbanks
to escape the oncoming sea.

RIVER DUDDON
Cumbria

xx

The old inventive Poets, had they seen,
Or rather felt, the entrancement that detains
Thy waters Duddon! 'mid these flowery plains;
The still repose, the liquid lapse serene,
Transferred to bowers imperishably green,
Had beautiful Elysium! But these chains
Will soon be broken; – a rough course remains,
Rough as the past; where Thou, of placid mien,
Innocuous as a firstling of the flock,
And countenanced like a soft cerulean sky,
Shalt change thy temper; and, with many a shock
Given and received in mutual jeopardy,
Dance, like a Bacchanal, from rock to rock,
Tossing her frantic thyrsus wide and high!

xxvi

Return, Content! for fondly I pursued,
Even when a child, the Streams – unheard, unseen;
Through tangled woods, impending rocks between;
Or, free as air, with flying inquest viewed
The sullen reservoirs whence their bold brood –
Pure as the morning, fretful, boisterous, keen,
Green as the salt-sea billows, white and green –
Poured down the hills, a choral multitude!

*This is only part of a long poem to the Duddon by Wordsworth, in which it
is described from its source down to the sea. Verses twenty and twenty-six do not therefore
refer to the same place. However, the vision they generated for me was of a
widening river, which danced like a choral multitude in drunken revelry. The location
could be at any suitable point along the lower reaches of the river, so the
problem was how to portray this vision. I interpreted it as a seething, almost
indistinguisable mass, with no predictable pattern. Water is perhaps best
photographed at shutter speeds of between 1/4 and 1/30 of a second, which gives varying
degrees of blur to promote the sense of movement. However, this still retains
an orderliness, which I didn't want. I decided therefore, as the location would look like
rapids seen through a series of rocks, to work at shutter speeds in excess of
five seconds, but no more than twenty-five seconds, after which fast-flowing water tends
to be reproduced more as a cloud.*

LITTLE LANGDALE
Lake District

...all at once, behold!
Beneath our feet, a little lowly vale,
Among the mountains; even as if the spot
Had been from eldest time by wish of theirs
So placed, to be shut out from all the world!
Urn-like it was in shape, deep as an urn;
With rocks encompassed, save that to the south
Was one small opening, where a heath-clad ridge
Supplied a boundary less abrupt and close;
A quiet treeless nook, with two green fields,
A liquid pool that glittered in the sun,
And one bare dwelling; one abode, no more!
It seemed the home of poverty and toil,
Though not of want; the little fields, made green
By husbandry of many thrifty years,
Paid cheerful tribute to the moorland house.

This is one of my favourite places, and I welcomed the chance to walk there
again. It was a beautiful morning following a night of rain, and as I slowly climbed I
realised I had a choice of several angles to produce a suitable composition.
The final ingredient, the sheep, was at first an unwilling participant – every time I moved
to include it, it moved out of view. I moved, it moved: it eventually acceded
to my request at the threat of a jar of mint sauce – hence the sheepish expression!

LODORE FALLS
Lake District

Dividing and gliding and sliding,
And falling and brawling and sprawling,
And driving and riving and striving,
And sprinkling and twinkling and wrinkling,
And sounding and bounding and rounding,
And bubbling and troubling and doubling,
And grumbling and rumbling and tumbling,
And clattering and battering and shattering.

Retreating and beating and meeting and sheeting,
Delaying and straying and playing and spraying,
Advancing and prancing and glancing and dancing,
Recoiling, turmoiling, and toiling and boiling,
And gleaming and streaming and steaming and beaming,
And rushing and flushing and brushing and gushing,
And curling and whirling and purling and twirling,
And thumping and plumping and bumping and jumping,
And dashing and flashing and splashing and clashing:
And so never ending, but always descending,
Sounds and motions for ever and ever are blending,
All at once and all o'er, with a mighty uproar,
And this way the Water comes down at Lodore.

*Southey's perception of the characteristics of the movement of water is so detailed, and
his communication of those observations through the written word is superb. The whole piece has
the rhythm of flowing water: you can almost imagine the Falls cascading from the page.
The illustration had to have a quality that made each viewing relate to the poem in a different
way. At first glance, the water would seem to be sprinkling and twinkling, the next, it
would seem to be splashing and clashing. A monumental task. I wanted a section of the location
which had a variation in the size of the water drop, and in the speed and volume of the
flow, with a pool below. I then had to compromise on a shutter speed which would blur the faster
flows, while almost freezing the slower. It required the greatest application of all that
I have learned in the past years.*

PAVY ARC
Lake District

when the mountain tops are shrouded
in a cold
clammy mist
or jagged peaks so stark
seem strangely soft
when sun kissed
when driving rain beats
incessantly
upon boulders
silver grey
or pinnacles shimmer
majestically
in the heat of summer's day
when the ridges disappear
under the winter's snow white gown
or the lower slopes vibrate

with a life of moorland green and brown
when crevasses and gulleys
tower upward
forboding
mean
or waters
from the heights
gush down
in crystal streams
when i walk and see
all these
for which we care
i will think of you
and feel your presence
there

*Although it may seem presumptuous to include one of my poems amidst the
work of some of the greatest literary figures this island has produced, it is done for a reason
far removed from self-glorification. During the production of this book,
a friend of mine tragically died on Scafell. Though I had known John Ripley and his wife
Meriel for only a relatively short time, they 'adopted' me when I first met
them, and since then had become my 'second parents'. John's experience of and love for
the mountains of Britain, which he happily shared with all who were interested,
coupled with his giant personality, endeared him to everyone he came into contact with.
He was much loved and respected, and will be very sadly missed by all who
knew him. This poem, and the illustration of one of his favourite high places will, I hope,
be a tribute to him.*

STYE HEAD TARN
Lake District

No one hurried them. The day was grey and still with little pools of sunlight in a dark sky. The hills had snow on their tops, but in the valleys the larches were beginning to break into intense green flame. As they wound up the Pass, the hills gathered about them, not grandly and with arrogant indifference as larger hills do in other countries, but with intimacy and friendliness as though they liked human beings and were interested in their fates.

By the Stye Head Tarn it was grim and desolate. This Tarn lies, an ebony unreflecting mirror, at the foot of the Gavel – beyond it, to the left, soft green ridges run to Esk Hause and the Langdales and lonely Eskdale. Above the green stretches there are the harsh serrated lines of Scafell Pike and the thin edge of Mickeldore. It was here however, and on this day that David had his first consciousness of the Gavel, the grand and noble hill that was one day to watch him struggling for his life. It was not to be seen at its finest here from the Tarn, for it sprawled away to the right almost without shape or form; nevertheless the spirit of it, dauntless, generous and wise, seized and held him. The sunlight, hidden elsewhere, broke above its head and caressed it; long strathes of water, blue like the cold spring streams that ran below the snowdrops, spread about its shoulders.

The whole expanse of land here is wide and strong, so that although no plan or form is visible, it makes of itself a form, the Tarn, the green stretches, the grouping hills having their own visible life without any human thought or agency to assist them.

Unfortunately, I missed the snow on the tops, and the grey sky refused to break out in rashes of blue. I was determined that the tarn should look ebony and unreflecting – it would have been pointless to trek up the pass in bright sunshine. I took a walk along the water's edge until the composition seemed right, which necessitated a paddle – not a pleasant task in the Lake District in January!

LOCH KATRINE
Western Highlands

And now, to issue from the glen,
No pathway meets the wanderer's ken,
Unless he climb, with footing nice,
A far projecting precipice.
The broom's tough roots his ladder made,
The hazel saplings lent their aid;
And thus an airy point he won,
Where, gleaming with the setting sun,
One burnish'd sheet of living gold,
Loch Katrine lay beneath him roll'd;
In all her length far winding lay,
With promontory, creek, and bay,
And islands that, empurpled bright,
Floated amid the livelier light,
And mountains, that like giants stand,
To sentinel enchanted land.
High on the south, huge BenVenue
Down to the lake in masses threw
Crags, knolls, and mounds, confusedly hurl'd,
The fragments of an earlier world:
A wildering forest feather'd o'er
His ruin'd sides and summit hoar.
While on the north, through middle air,
Ben-an heaved high his forehead bare.

*Anyone who has visited this loch cannot fail to be disturbed by its extensive
commercialisation at the hands of the local water authority, and the exploitation of what is, after
all, a natural commodity. More upsetting still are the many signs which threaten
punishment against those who deviate from the unsightly concrete road which snakes its way along
the shore. I sincerely believe that no area should be forbidden to the serious nature
lover, provided he or she takes great care not to damage or disturb the environment. Finding
Scott's viewpoint meant a scramble through rocks and trees. I waited patiently until
the sun broke through the cloud, constantly fearing the iron hand of authority, which could come
to rest upon my guilt-ridden shoulders at any moment.*

GLENCOE
Western Highlands

ometimes we walked, sometimes ran; and as it drew on to morning, walked ever less and ran the more. For all our hurry, day began to come in while we were still far from any shelter. It found us in a prodigious valley, strewn with rocks and where ran a foaming river. Wild mountains stood around it; there grew neither grass nor trees; and I have sometimes thought since then, that it may have been the valley called Glencoe, where the massacre was in the time of King William.

Then I saw why we had come there; for the two rocks, being both somewhat hollow on the top, and sloping one to the other, made a kind of dish or saucer, where as many as three or four men might have lain hidden. All this while Alan had not said a word, and had run and climbed with such a savage, silent frenzy of hurry, that I knew he was in mortal fear of some miscarraige. Even now we were on the rock he said nothing, nor so much as relaxed the frowning look upon his face; but clapped flat down, and keeping only one eye above the edge of our place of shelter scouted all round the compass. The dawn had come quite clear; we could see the stony sides of the valley, and its bottom, which was bestrewed with rocks, and the river, which went from one side to the other, and made white falls; but nowhere the smoke of a house, nor any living creature, but some eagles screaming round a cliff.

*Most people feel that this place is a sinister, foreboding valley, threatening
treachery, even death: an impression perpetuated by most photography, my own included,
which tends to be produced in bad weather or using mystery-enhancing
techniques like grainy film. On re-reading the novel, it came as a pleasant surprise to
discover that the fugitives flee through this place in bright conditions. I knew
from experience that a permanent funereal shroud of mist and rain often hangs over this
area, providing an attractive atmosphere for the visitor. So the challenge was
all the greater, for not only had I to catch the sun, but I also wanted to retain some of the
dark atmosphere with deep shadowed areas. I opted for the latter, and a walk
along the old drover's road brought me to just such a hollow, over which men might have
watched their pursuers.*

BEN NEVIS
Western Highlands

Presently they set out northward again; and he told her the names of the various mountains – those giant masses whose sterile altitudes, rising far above the sparsely wooded slopes and precipices, seemed to recede away from human ken; although along their base, here and there, was some narrow strip of cultivation – a field with the hay gathered into cocks (for, summer – like as the day was, they were now at the end of August), or a patch of yellowing corn just over the deep sapphire of the sea. Then, when they had got through the Narrows of Corran, they came in sight of the mighty bulk of Ben Nevis, towering high above the lower hills of bracken and heather, its vast shoulders of granite seamed with rose-pink scaurs, that caught a warm glow from the now westering sun. A brisk breeze had sprung up by this time from the north or north-west, driving the sea around them into a vivid blue; and far away beyond these lapping waters, on the shore, amid some soft green foliage, were two or three white dots of houses; these were the outskirts of Fort William.

Undoubtedly the jewel in the Highland crown, like a diamond Ben Nevis has many facets, depending upon the route of your approach. From the north and east it looks impressive enough, though its vast bulk is somewhat reduced in appearance by the attendant lower mountains. The Ben's true majesty can only be properly appreciated when it stands alone above the loch and the town of Fort William. It was essential to pursue this angle, though I had to avoid an unoriginal photograph, for this is the first view that most tourists see, and is also the one which pulls the disc cameras out of their cases. I crossed to the far side of the loch, to include it in an early-morning photograph. An early-evening shot would have been just as effective, giving the granite a pinker glow and a shadowy foreground, to focus attention on the mountain.

ARDNAMURCHAN PENINSULA
West Coast of Scotland

Along peninsula of solid rock,
upholstered every year in threadbare green.
Stones everywhere, ambigious and burgeoning.
In Sanna ramparts of them
march around our crofts
but whether to keep cattle out or other stones
no man can say.
And at Kilchoan there were three houses
cropped from one field.
That was when I was a boy.
The masons left the pebbles
and there's a castle now, waiting to be harvested.
God was short of earth when he made Ardnamurchan.

The last line of this poem provided the initial basis for this illustration.
I thought it was a brilliant, yet simple statement, which set my thought patterns into
overdrive about one of the few areas of Scotland that I had never
visited. My impression was of an almost barren peninsula, made of cold, hard, unyielding
stone, with the barest minimum of fertile soil. The best way to capture the
feeling behind the description was to portray it in very dark grey or black tones which, on
colour film, meant a deep silhouette against a bright sky. Since it was a
peninsula, a fluid foreground mirroring the sky would enhance the effect.

NEAR GLENELG
West Coast of Scotland

The sea took up where the burn left off, and its foreshore formed the whole frontage of the field, running up nearest to me into a bay of rocks and sand.

To the north and south the coast is rock for the most part, but opening here and there to long gravel beaches which the prevailing westerly gales pile high with the sea's litter. It is a fierce shoreline, perilous with reef and rock, and Camusfeàrna with its snow white sandy beaches, green close-cropped turf, and low white lighthouse has a welcoming quality enhanced by the dark rugged coastline on either side. It is a coast of cliffs and of caves, deep commodious caves that have their entrances, for the most part, well above the tide's level, for over the centuries the sea has receded, and between the cliffs the shingle of its old beaches lies bare.

As I have already mentioned in my Introduction, this book provided the original inspiration for Literary Landscapes. The area is quite difficult to reach: now I realise why Gavin Maxwell required a Land Rover. With today's saloons, it is kinder to exhaust systems to park and walk. What's more, Forestry Commission padlocks are not easy to pick! It remains just as it was, except sadly, Camusfeàrna is no more. After the fire, the house was demolished, and there remains only a stone at the site, under which lie the ashes of the author. I knew the area quite well, and so had many preconceived plans for the illustration. The lighthouse, perhaps, or the caves, or the rocks of the shoreline? During my trek along the beach I recalled the mention of the sea's litter, and there it was, at my feet. Rotting planks, tree branches, pebbles, seaweed, all swept into a natural design by the waves. Perhaps the spirit of Edal the otter still plays amongst it.

THE CUILLINS
Isle of Skye

The individuality of The Coolins is not seen in their summits, which are often almost ugly, but in the colour of the rocks, the atmospheric effects, the relative largeness and harmony of the details compared with the actual size of the mountains, and most of all in the mountain mystery that wraps them round: not the mystery of clearness, such as is seen in the Alps and Himalayas, where range recedes into the infinite distance till the white snow peaks cannot be distinguished from the clouds, but in the obscure and secret beauty born of the mists, the rain, and the sunshine in a quiet and untroubled land, no longer vexed by the rude and violent manifestations of the active powers of nature.

When the wild Atlantic storms sweep across the mountaings; when the streams gather in volume, and the bare rock faces are streaked with the foam of a thousand waterfalls; when the wind shrieks amongst the rock pinnacles, and sky, loch, and hillside in one dull grey, the Coolin can be savage and dreary indeed; perhaps though the clouds towards the evening may break, then the torn masses of vapour, tearing in mad hunt along the ridges, will be lit by the rays of the sun slowly descending in the western sea, 'robing the gloom with a vesture of divers colours, of which the threads are purple and scarlet, and the embroideries flame'; and as the light flashes from the black rocks, and the shadows deepen in the corries, the superb beauty, the melancholy, the mystery of these mountains of the Isle of Mist will be revealed. But the golden glory will melt from off the mountains, the light that silvered the great slabs will slowly fail, from out the corries darkness heralding the black night will creep with stealthy tread hiding all in gloom; and last of all, behind the dark luminous, jagged, and fantastic outline of the Coolins the glittering stars will flash out from the clear sky, no wind will stir the great quiet, only the far-off sound, born of the rhythmic murmur of the sea waves beating on the rock bound shore of lonely Scavaig, remains as a memory of the storm.

What intrigued me about this passage is that it was written by a climber: there is a sense of feeling, rather than mere observation. It is almost as though the author is part of the mountains and vice versa, which seems natural, since he spent so much time climbing those ridges. My original intention was to illustrate a scene from one of the summits, but no climbing friends were available at the time, and to ascend alone would be sheer insanity: this range is extremely hostile, even in the most perfect conditions. I decided instead to show the range at its most awesome, at the same time showing its character and how unforgiving it can be to those who attempt its slopes as a jaunt. The most suitable location, from Glen Slighachan, displays the splendour of its winter coat, which is often missed. The conditions were perfect, as the brightness range, too great for transparency, material, meant that by exposing the snow and water, the rocks would be shadow. This accentuated the mountain range, making them seem even more dramatic.

LOCH CORUISK
Isle of Skye

The ground on which we walked was the margin of a lake, which seemed to have sustained the constant ravage of torrents from these rude neightbours. The shores consisted of huge strata of naked granite, here and there intermixed with bogs, and heaps of gravel, and sand piled in the empty water courses. Vegetation there was little or none; and the mountains rose so perpendicularly from the water edge, that Borrowdale, or even Glencoe, is a jest to them. We proceeded a mile and a half up this deep, dark, and solitary lake, which was about two miles long, half a mile broad, and is, as we learned, of extreme depth....

The proper name is Loch Corrieskin, from the deep corrie, or hollow, in the mountains of Cuilin, which affords the basin for this wonderful sheet of water. It is as exquisite a savage scene as Loch Katrine is a scene of romantic beauty. After having penetrated so far as distinctly to observe the termination of the lake under an immense precipice which rises abruptly from the water, we returned....

Stones, or rather large masses and fragments of rocks of a composite kind, perfectly different from the strata of the lake, were scattered upon the bare rocky beach, in the strangest and most precarious situations, as if abandoned by the torrents upon the ledges of the natural rock, with so little security, that the slightest push moved them, though their weight might exceed many tons....

The opposite side of the lake seemed quite pathless and inaccessible, as the huge mountain, one of the detached ridges of the Cuilin hills, sinks in a profound and perpendicular precipice down to the water. On the left hand side, which we traversed, rose a higher and equally inaccessible mountain, the top of which strongly resembled the shivered crater of an exhausted volcano....

Upon the whole, though I have seen many scenes of more extensive desolation, I have never witnessed any in which it pressed more deeply upon the eye and the heart that at Loch Corrieskin; at the same time that its grandeur elevated and redeemed it from the wild and dreary character of utter barrenness.

I had visited this loch many times, and was amazed by its barrenness. The amphitheatre of the Cuillins looks down with vertical menace onto the land-locked water that was once part of the sea. It was one of only two occasions when, having the photograph already, I searched for a suitable description. I knew there would be few problems, since it had been a source of pilgrimage and inspiration for many writers and illustrators of the nineteenth century. Eventually, I decided that Scott's poem, Lord of the Isles, *was the most atmospheric. The library copy I had originally read was unavailable, but while waiting for its return to the shelves, a friend offered me the use of what had been his father's copy. What treasure I found, by chance – a copy of the 1833 editition, complete with Scott's notes about his journey to the Isle of Skye. The notes, I thought, were even more descriptive than the poem.*

ABOVE PLOCKTON
West Coast of Scotland

The loch, though ultimately leading to the open sea, is in appearance completely landlocked. Its entrance is closed by the island of Skye, which sprawls like a starfish between us and the Altantic. The loch itself is double faced: its salt and tidal waters, its fish, shells, and weed proclaim it sea, while the unbroken circle of hills and the calm surface in which they are often reflected, suggest an inland lake. In this, the western section, it is four miles wide, and as the nearest hills are nowhere very high, it has not the oppressive gloom of many narrower lochs, and is fairly free from dangerous and sudden squalls.

The best general notion of the loch is got by climbing under the face of the crags that overhang its southern shore, until, perched on a ledge eight hundred feet above, you see its whole extent spread chart-like at your feet. On a clear day at low tide every detail is plain. The bays, promontories, and islands…

The appearance of all these islands varies with the state of the tide. At the highest springs, their rocky spurs and promontories and the fringe of half-submerged reefs and skerries are lost to sight, and the grassy tops look almost awash. Six hours later, especially when viewed from sea level, the flat green isle has become a craggy plateau, flanked by jagged fangs, and surrounded by weed-covered rocks.

I had read this book before I began collating material for Literary Landscapes, *my attention being brought to it in a rather roundabout way. Whilst in Ireland, I made my protest against our government, who feel it is their responsibility to censor what we read, and bought a copy of* Spycatcher. *The author, Peter Wright, once assisted Margaret Leigh on the Highland farm which she had intended to be a training centre for London slum boys. This description is of the adjacent sea loch, typical of so many on the West Coast which I have had the pleasure of exploring. At the end of a hard day's toil, one of the compensations of living on such a remote farm must have been the frequent, breathtaking sunsets that visit this coast.*

NORTHERN SCOTLAND

The little Highland community in which Kenn lived was typical of what might be found anywhere around the northern and western shores of Scotland; the river coming down out of the wooded glen or strath into the little harbour; the sloping croft lands, with their small cultivated fields: the croft houses here and there, with an odd one on a far ridge against the sky: the school, the post office, and the old church, where the houses herded loosely into a township; and inland the moors lifting to blue mountains.

A resilience to all the violent attacks of oceans and elements has been developed not only by the natural coastline here, but also by the communities which nestle along the shore. I think the author probably drew upon characteristics for various places to mould into one fictitious village. In this typical scene, I tried to capture the essence of a close, harmonious community; an atmosphere that Gunn must have intended to convey. Strangely enough, only a few miles from the scene was what looked like an enormous petrol station for naval ships, and the infamous Gruinard Island, lying only yards offshore, the location of the anthrax experiments which have made it uninhabitable for the last forty years or so. It amazes me how man always manages to cast a dark shadow over even the most isolated and idyllic of territories.

LOCH MONAR
Highlands

Breasting the crest of this hard-won windswept pass, swing to the right and you journey in a matter of years into a land transformed. It is perhaps the most breath-catching shift of scenery in the north. Highland grandeur stretching before you in its finest form. Away to the distant blueness of a heat-shimmering summer's day glitter the shining waters of Loch Monar. Tree-clad tapering promontories run out in rock and sand to its tranquil depths. The eye is drawn hungrily to the wide amphitheatre of hills, ridge upon ridge, with the tall sharp peak of Bidean an Eoin Deirg rising majestically above Strathmore and gracing the scene. 'High top of the red bird', all its splendour of deep corrie and ageless rock discernible over a long distance in clear weather. Here Strathfarrar is at its widest, a full ten miles as the crow flies from the serrated north ridges to the south marches and the great reposing bulk of An Riabhachan, highest hill in Ross-shire. A vast scene of high shapely hills entwined with river and lochan, woods and corries which long hold the gaze of those with a feeling for wild places. By and by one would look down to the more immediate surroundings and the pleasant pine and larch bordered croftland of Monar itself. The grey stone lodge nesting snugly amongst the trees: a burn, noisy with falls and pools, at its side door. A thoughtfully planted avenue of pine trunks framed the view from the front lodge windows. Out it led, over to an old thatched boathouse at the margin of the loch, out and away, away to the far peaks of stirring memory for the irresistible stalking days.

I came upon this book purely by chance while browsing through the library shelves, and was attracted by its cover. The story it contained was an accurate and well-portrayed tale of the hard life in one of the more hostile and remote areas of this island. The loch's approaches are privately owned, yet the Spencer Nairn and Lovitt estates, who own parts of the drive, allow easy access – an action which should be loudly applauded in the days when vast tracts of our heritage are being closed by their owners. At the time I visited, there were literally hundreds of deer grazing within feet of me. The loch is now dammed, so all that remains of the once-mighty falls is a chasm and a trickle. Rain fell incessantly, and I was glad not to have to tramp the hills herding a flock of far-flung sheep. The tree stumps amazed me, for they were so easily moved. It seemed that long immersion had made them as light as balsa wood, and one of my souvenirs is a branch shaped like an antler.

FALLS OF FOYERS
Loch Ness, Scotland

Among the healthy hills and ragged woods
The roaring Fyers pours his mossy floods;
Till full he dashes on the rocky mounds,
Where, thro' a shapeless breach, his stream resounds.
As high in air the bursting torrents flow,
As deep recoiling surges foam below,
Prone down the rock the whitening sheet descends,
And viewless Echo's ear, astonished, rends.
Dim-seen, thro' rising mists and ceaseless showers,
The hoary cavern, wide-surrounding, lowers.
Still thro' the gap the struggling river toils.
And still, below, the horrid cauldron boils.

I find the term 'falls' can be a bit of a misnomer, since the object is
often nowhere near as spectacular as the name suggests. The Falls of Foyers, however,
with their whitening sheet and echoing sounds, promised something special.
It is a difficult place to find, being on the opposite shore of Loch Ness to the main tourist
route, reachable via single-track roads. But neither this inconvenience,
nor the short, steep path of a viewing platform should in any way deter lovers of waterfalls
from a visit. It is as stunning and spectacular as the poem suggests.

RANNOCH MOOR
Grampians

I stood on the hillock clothed with its stunted saughtrees and waited for the day that was mustering somewhere to the east, far from the frozen sea of moss and heather tuft. A sea more lonely than any ocean the most wide and distant, where no ship heaves, and no isle lifts beckoning trees above the level of the waves: a sea soundless, with no life below its lamentable surface, no little fish or proud leviathan plunging and romping and flashing from the silver roof of fretted wave dishevelled to the deep profound. The moorfowl does not cry there, the coney has no habitation. It rolled, the sea so sour, so curdled, from my feet away to mounts I knew by day stupendous and not so far, but now in the dark so hid that they were but troubled clouds upon the distant marge.

The grey day crept above the land: I watched it from my hillock, and I shrunk in my clothing that seemed so poor a shielding in a land so chill. A cold clammy dawn, that never cleared even as it aged, but held a hint of mist to come that should have warned me of the danger I faced in venturing on the untravelled surface of the moor, even upon its safer verge.

I was well out on Rannoch before the day was full awake on the country, walking at great trouble upon the coarse barren soil, among rotten bog grass, lichened stones, and fir-roots that thrust from the black peat like skeletons of antiquity. And then I came on a cluster of lochs – grey, cold, vagrant lochs – still to some degree in the thrall of frost. Here's one who has ever a fancy for such lochans, that are lost and sobbing, sobbing, even on among the hills, where the reeds and the rushes hiss in the wind, and the fowls with sheeny feather make night and day cheery with their call. But not those lochs of Rannoch, those black basins crumbling at the edge of a rotten soil. I skirted them as far off as I could, as though they were the lochans of a nightmare that drag the traveller into their kelpie tenants' arms.

Rannoch Moor is another area I knew quite well from previous travels,
and this passage sums up exactly the characteristics I remember. Before I journeyed onto
the moor, I had set my target scene for the photograph, in which most of
what is described could either be seen or imagined. It would be a relatively easy
illustration, owing to the nature of the terrain – the only dilemma
would be which angle to choose. Providing that the usual precautions were taken, it would
not be a dangerous hike, since the mist was beginning to lift when I set out.
I hope the photograph and the passage speak for themselves.

BY NORTH BERWICK
Lothian

As we had first made inland, so our road came in the end to lie very near due north; the old Kirk of Aberlady for a landmark on the left; on the right, the top of Berwick Law; and it was thus we struck the shore again, not far from Dirleton. From North Berwick west to Gillane Ness there runs a string of four small islets, Craiglieth, the Lamb, Fidra, and Eyebrough, notable by their diversity of size and shape. Fidra is the most particular, being a strange grey islet of two humps, made the more conspicuous by a piece of ruin; and I mind that (as we drew closer to it) by some door or window of these ruins the sea peeped through like some man's eye....

The shore in face of these islets is altogether waste. Here is no dwelling of man, and scarce any passage, or at most of vagabond children running at their play. Gillane is a small place on the far side of the Ness, the folk of Dirleton go to their business in the inland fields, and those of North Berwick straight to the sea-fishing from their haven; so that few parts of the coast are lonelier. But I mind as we crawled upon our bellies into that multiplicity of heights and hollows, keeping a bright eye upon all sides, and our hearts hammering at our ribs, there was such a shining of the sun and the sea, such a stir of the wind in the bent grass, and such a bustle of down-popping rabbits and up-flying gulls, that the desert seemed to me like a place alive....

That part of the beach was long and flat, and excellent walking when the tide was down; a little cressy burn flowed over it in one place to the sea and the sandhills ran along the head of it like the rampart of a town.

A chase sequence from the pen of Robert Louis Stevenson shows how he
loved to place fugitives and their pursuers in the wild waste-lands of his native Scotland.
I approached the coast on a cold, blustery afternoon. It was certainly a
desolate area, well chosen by the author, though it seems to have become a popular
exercise area for humans and animals alike. It was most suitable for
my original idea of allowing the camera to become the eyes of the pursued. I crawled
around at ground level, making appearances through the long grass
at regular intervals, much to the consternation of the Sunday strollers. I thought the worst
risk of this position was coming face to face with a rabbit: a mouthful of sand
soon told me I was wrong!

LINDISFARNE
Northumberland

The castle with its battled walls,
The ancient Monastery's halls,
A solemn, huge, and dark red pile,
Plac'd on the margin of the isle.

In Saxon strength that Abbey frown'd,
With massive arches broad and round,
That rose alternate, row and row,
On ponderous columns, short and low,
Built ere the art was known,
By pointed aisle, and shafted stalk,
The arcades of an alley'd walk
To emulate in stone.
On the deep walls, the heathen Dane
Had pour'd his impious rage in vain;
and needful was such strength to these

Expos'd to the tempestuous seas,
Scourg'd by the winds' eternal sway,
Open to rovers fiece as they,
Which could twelve hundred years withstand
Winds, waves, and northern pirates' hand.
Not but that portions of the pile,
Rebuilded in a later style,
Show'd where the spoilers' hand had been;
Not but the wasting sea-breeze keen
Had worn the pillar's carving quaint,
And moulder'd in his niche the saint,
And rounded, with consuming power,
The pointed angles of each tower;
Yes still entire the Abbey stood,
Like veteran, worn, but unsubdu'd.

*I had visited Lindisfarne before, so it was necessary to clear my mind of all
preconceptions before I read Scott's description. I then had to list the attributes of the
castle which the poem conveys. The castle was elevated, proudly standing,
ageless and unbowed in resistance to all the rigours that humanity and nature had
subjected it to over the centuries. I was then able to recall the location
as I remembered it, and from that deliberate my approach. The elevated proudness would
require a low viewpoint, and to further emphasize this feature it needed
to be outlined against a threatening sky. The agelessness would have to be portrayed by
contrast with something decayed. Rocks and modern buildings would
be of no use, so the final ingredient could not be selected until I was in situ. As it turned
out, the piles – the remnants of a jetty – appeared to be barely resisting
the ravages of the elements.*

CHILLINGHAM
Northumberland

O the high valley, the little low hill,
    And the cornfield over the sea,
The wind that rages and then lies still,
    And the clouds that rest and flee!

O the grey island in the rainbow haze,
    And the long thin spits of land,
The roughening pastures and the stony ways,
    And the golden flash of sand.

O the red heather on the moss-wrought rock,
    And the fir-tree stiff and straight,
The shaggy old sheep-dog barking at the flock,
    And the rotten old five barred gate!

O the brown bracken, the blackberry bough,
    The scent of gorse in the air!
I shall love them as ever I love them now,
    I shall weary in heaven to be there!

*I had difficulty finding Chillingham Hill at first, which may explain why
the RAF turned me down when, as a schoolboy, I applied to be a pilot. After clambering
to the top the signs told me that I was on the way to Ros Castle, which I
found a comfort. Having decided that this was going to be a general view, the castle would
increase my choices. The castle, however, was only about eight feet square,
and the walls were no more than four feet high. The disappointment I felt increased when
I discovered that the vista towards the coast, though beautiful to the eye,
was photographically a non-starter. The view in the other direction towards the Cheviots
held some promise. Past experience of the moods of the clouds made me
almost certain that there would be a brief opening with a low sun breaking through. My
patience was rewarded, though the movement of the clouds meant that I
had only seconds when the fields were illuminated as I wanted them.*

AUTHORS

Richard Adams
1920-

Harrison Ainsworth
1805-1882

Matthew Arnold
1822-1888

Sabine Baring-Gould
1834-1924

Bernard Barton
1784-1849

Sir John Betjemen
1906-1984

W. Black
1841-1898

George Borrow
1803-1881

Charlotte Brontë
1816-1855

Emily Brontë
1818-1848

Robert Burns
1759-1796

Mary Coleridge
1861-1907

Norman Collie
1859-1942

George Crabbe
1754-1832

C. Day-Lewis
1904-1972

Charles Dickens
1812-1870

Daphne Du Maurier
1907-1989

George Eliot
1819-1880

Robin Flower
1881-1946

John Fowles
1926-

Mrs. Gaskell
1810-1866

Thomas Gray
1716-1771

Neil M. Gunn
1891-1973

Thomas Hardy
1840-1928

Charles Kingsley
1819-1875

D. H. Lawrence
1885-1930

Margaret Leigh
1894-

Richard Llewellyn
1906-1983

Alisdair Maclean
1926-

Gavin Maxwell
1914-1969

Sir Lewis Morris
1833-1907

N. Munro
1864-1930

George Orwell
1903-1950

Thomas Love Peacock
1785-1866

Eden Phillpotts
1862-1960

Sir Walter Scott
1771-1832

Robert Southey
1774-1843

Michael J. Stead
1952-

Robert Louis Stevenson
1850-1894

Bram Stoker
1847-1912

Charles Swinburne
1837-1909

Alfred, Lord Tennyson
1809-1892

Dylan Thomas
1914-1953

Iain R. Thomson
1933-

Leo Walmsley
1892-1963

Hugh Walpole
1884-1941

William Wordsworth
1770-1850

W. B. Yeats
1865-1939

ACKNOWLEDGEMENTS

The author would like to acknowledge the following sources:

P10 From *Three Fevers* by Leo Walmsley (Collins)

P24 From *Country Child* by Alison Uttley (Faber & Faber)

P44 From *Watership Down* by Richard Adams (Penguin. Reproduced with the permission of David Higham Associates Ltd.)

P48 From *The French Lieutenant's Woman* by John Fowles (Reproduced with the permission of Anthony Sheil Associates)

P50 & 52 From *Children of the Mist* by Eden Phillpotts (Reproduced with the permission of The Royal Literary Fund)

P56 From *Sir John Betjeman: Collected Poems* (John Murray)

P60 From *Jamaica Inn* by Daphne Du Maurier (Reproduced with the permission of Curtis Brown Ltd., London, on behalf of the Estate of Daphne Du Maurier)

P66 From *How Green Was My Valley* by Richard Llewellyn (Michael Joseph. © 1939 by the Estate of Richard Llewellyn.)

P68 From *Under Milk Wood* by Dylan Thomas (Dent. Reproduced with the permission of David Higham Associates Ltd.)

P80 From *The Room* by C. Day-Lewis (Jonathan Cape. Reproduced with the permission of The Executive of the Estate of C. Day-Lewis.)

P82 From *The Road to Wigan Pier* by George Orwell (Reproduced with the permission of the Estate of the late Sonia Brownwell Orwell, and Martin Secker and Warburg)

P96 From *Rogue Herries* by Hugh Walpole (Macmillan)

P104 From *From the Wilderness* by Alisdair Maclean (Gollancz)

P106 From *Ring of Bright Water* by Gavin Maxwell (Penguin. © 1960 by Gavin Maxwell Enterprises Ltd.)

P114 From *Highland River* by Neil M. Gunn (Arrow Books)

P116 From *Isolation Shepherd* by Iain R. Thomson (Bidean Books)

Thanks also to my mother, father, and Kate for their support and encouragement, to Lorraine for all her efforts as an unpaid assistant and to the staff at Scarborough Library for their diligence and patience in assisting me in my research.

Thanks also to everyone else not mentioned by name, who may have helped with suggestions, a bed for the night on my travels, or in any other way.